THE
WILLIAM BARCLAY
PRAYER BOOK

THE
WILLIAM BARCLAY
PRAYER BOOK

Edited by Ronnie Barclay

Fount

An Imprint of HarperCollins*Publishers*

Fount Paperbacks is an Imprint of
HarperCollins*Religious*
Part of HarperCollins*Publishers*
77–85 Fulham Palace Road, London W6 8JB

The material in this book first appeared
in *The Plain Man's Book of Prayers*

© William Barclay 1959, *More Prayers for the Plain Man*
© William Barclay 1962, and *Prayers for Help and Healing*
© William Barclay 1968, all published by Fontana
and subsequently by Fount Paperbacks

This book first published in Great Britain
in 1994 by Fount Paperbacks

1 3 5 7 9 10 8 6 4 2

Copyright in the compilation © 1994 Ronnie Barclay

Ronnie Barclay asserts the moral right to be
identified as the compiler of this work

A catalogue record for this book is available
from the British Library

ISBN 0 00 627862-0

Typeset by Harper Phototypesetters Limited
Northampton, England
Printed and bound in Great Britain by
Mackays of Chatham PLC, Chatham, Kent

CONTENTS

FOREWORD

My father, William Barclay, was born in Wick in Caithness in North Scotland on 5th December 1907. His theology was created in a happy, privileged home and he experienced the security of growing up under the care of intelligent, contented parents. Theologically, his parents were strictly conservative and, despite later criticisms of being 'too liberal', he never stopped believing that his main aim in life was to win souls for Christ.

William Barclay had an excellent school and university record, and in 1932 his path was set for a long and distinguished career when he completed his studies with the award of a BD with distinction at the University of Glasgow. He was minister of Trinity Church, Renfrew, on the Clydeside for fourteen years and it was there that he acquired his outstanding communication skills. On 1st January 1947 he began a career as lecturer in New Testament Language and Literature at the University of Glasgow, the start of an era in which his name was to become known in almost every household in the land.

William Barclay's most important achievement is considered by many to be his 'Daily Study Bible Readings', now called *The Daily Study Bible*, a commentary on all of the books of the New Testament. However, he wrote over eighty books and there are translations in Afrikaans, Chinese, French, German, Indonesian, Japanese, Norwegian, Russian and Spanish. Countless people have been helped by my father's aim 'to make the life and words of Jesus live'. His television series were watched by everyone, not just church-goers, and did much to fulfil his ambition to 'bring Jesus to the unchurched masses'.

He received many honours: a DD from the University of Edinburgh; the CBE; the freedom of Motherwell and Wishaw (where he had spent his childhood and formative years); an Upper Room Citation. In 1963 he was appointed Professor to the

Chair of Divinity and Biblical Criticism at the University of Glasgow, where he remained until he retired in 1974.

My father suffered many tragedies throughout his life. At the age of five he was left partially deaf after an attack of scarlet fever. My sister, Barbara, was drowned in a tragic boating accident on 10th August 1956, only a few weeks after he had received the honour of his DD. In 1969 he was diagnosed as having emphysema and Parkinson's Disease, and was given eight years to live. The doctors were right and he died on 24th January 1978 in Glasgow. The title of his last book, *The Lord is my Shepherd*, published after his death, reveals the faith and trust in Jesus which he never lost, even in the dark, shadowy days.

William Barclay was a wonderful husband, father and grandfather, but above all he was Christ's man. 'The others we know about, Jesus we know. The others we remember, Jesus we experience', he loved to say. His favourite words came from Isaac Watts' hymn, words which he sang with his beloved Trinity College Choir at every concert they gave:

> *Were the whole realm of nature mine,*
> *That were an offering far too small:*
> *Love so amazing, so divine,*
> *Demands my soul, my life, my all.*

The prayers in this Anthology are taken from *The Plain Man's Book of Prayers, More Prayers for the Plain Man* and *Prayers for Help and Healing,* first published in 1959, 1962 and 1968 respectively. My father held strong views about prayer, and our enjoyment is enhanced by understanding them. The following reflections are based on his own writings about prayer.

William Barclay held the view that we are creatures of two worlds – of the visible world of space and time, but also of an unseen world which every now and again breaks in upon our consciousness. In the dark, for example, we feel that there is something there; or on a hilltop, on a lonely road, in the face of a sunset, in a cathedral or church.

We need help from outside to go on especially at times of crisis or sorrow. Even the agnostic prays reluctantly: 'O God, if there is a God, save my soul, if I have a soul!' Prayer is unquestionably the natural human reaction to a situation which is beyond us. Unfortunately we tend to connect prayer with the extraordinary, the abnormal, the moments when life goes disastrously wrong. Prayer should be a constant part of life. It is simply remembering that God is not only the rescuer, but the Friend with whom we live day by day.

What should our daily prayer be like? How should we pray? Jesus gives us the answer in the name which He gave to God: Abba, Father. This was the word by which the little Jewish child addressed his father in the family circle. We can talk to God with the same intimacy, confidence and trust as a little child uses when he talks to his father. We do not need to use any special kind of religious or theological language. We can stand, kneel, sit or lie down as we pray. It is all the same. God is still all-powerful and wonderful, but he has become for us the friend of all friends.

When should we pray? Paul said: 'Pray without ceasing' (1 Thessalonians 5:17). We can go to God at any time. We can never be a nuisance.

Where should we pray? There are certain places in which we are bound to feel closer to God than anywhere else, but the whole earth is the temple of God. We can pray anywhere, in our own room, on the street, in the train, on the bus, using, if we wish, 'arrow prayers' – words, phrases, half-sentences spoken anywhere to God. If God is everywhere, then we can meet him anywhere.

Why should we pray? Prayer is as much listening to God as it is talking to God, as much accepting his will as asking for what our will desires. Too many people say to God: 'Your will be changed', rather than 'Your will be done'. In all our prayers there should be a time of silence for listening.

What should we pray for? The test of any wish or desire or ambition or aim is – Can I pray for it? We can pray for anything for which we can really feel that it is right to ask God. We can tell God about problems which we cannot share with anyone else.

What can we expect from prayer? Prayer is not escape. Prayer is not flight, it is power. Prayer does not deliver us from some terrible situation; prayer enables us to face and master the situation. We are given the strength which is not our strength and we come out at the other side of our suffering, not simply a survivor, but with a faith that is strengthened and deepened. Prayer is not the easy way out. It is not a kind of Aladdin's lamp. It is a basic rule of prayer that God will never do for us what we can do for ourselves. Prayer must never be selfish. No one can pray to receive something which will cause someone else disappointment or loss. The greatest thing we can do is to pray for other people.

It has been said that an atheist is someone with no invisible means of support. To have to meet life with nothing more than we can bring to it is bound to be an experience which brings fear and defeat. In prayer we meet everything with God.

My father loved to tell a story which his father shared with him. My grandfather used to visit a girl suffering from an incurable disease. On one occasion he took with him a little book of comfort for those in trouble. He gave it to her. 'I know this book', said the girl. 'Have you got it already?', my grandfather asked. She smiled and answered quietly, 'I wrote it.' Prayer is this power to help others and through it nothing can separate us from the love of God in Christ Jesus our Lord.

RONNIE BARCLAY
February 1994

PREFACE
Ourselves and our prayers

It should not be difficult to pray, for prayer is the most natural activity in the world. William James, the American philosopher, said: 'Many reasons have been given why we should not pray, whilst others are given why we should. But in all this very little is said of the reason why we do pray. The reason why we pray is simply that we cannot help praying.' It is one of the most significant facts about the human situation that no tribe, however primitive, has been found who did not pray to such gods as they had. Prayer is not an acquired art; it is an instinct. When life is too much for us, when we are strained beyond breaking-point, tempted beyond the power to resist, when our minds are troubled, and our hearts are broken, then we pray.

If that be so, we may well ask: Why then do we need any help in prayer? If prayer is so natural, why cannot every man pray perfectly well for himself? Technique is not a word with very high and lofty associations, and yet there is a technique in everything. There can be nothing in this world so natural as breathing, and yet there is a technique in breathing; there is a right and a wrong way to breathe; and health will depend on which way we use. There are few activities so natural as walking; and yet there is a technique of walking. There is a right and a wrong way to walk, and it will make a very great difference which way we use.

We need to be taught how to use everything. It is quite possible for a person to possess something very precious, and yet to fail to get anything like the best out of it, because he or she is not using it properly. We have to learn how to use a typewriter or an electric razor; we have to learn how to tune a violin or a television set; we have to learn how to drive a motor car; we have to learn even how to cook food, and how to cook it in such a way that we will get the maximum benefit from it.

The simplest and most natural actions have their technique, and we have to learn how to use even our most precious possessions. It is the same with prayer. There are many people who in their childhood years were taught to pray in a kind of a way; but bit by bit, as the years went on, they drifted out of the habit of prayer; and, if they considered the matter, and were honest about it, they would probably say that they stopped praying because they had not found that prayer was any use. If that is so, the reason is that they were not praying in the right way; they had never learned and were never taught the technique of prayer; they possessed a very precious gift, but they did not know how to use it. Let us then look at some of the laws of prayer.

All prayer begins from the fact that God is even more ready to listen than we are to speak to him, and even more ready to give than we are to ask. When we pray, we do not go to a grudging and an unwilling God. God, as Paul saw it, has given proof, unanswerable proof, of his generosity. 'He that spared not his own Son, but delivered him up for us all, how shall he not with him also freely give us all things?' (Romans 8:32). There are two prayer parables which Jesus spoke, and their misunderstanding has done infinite harm. One is the Parable of the Friend at Midnight (Luke 11:5–8). It tells how a traveller arrived at a man's house. It was so late that the man had no food to set before him, and in the East hospitality is a sacred duty. So the man went to his neighbour, and knocked at his door in order to borrow bread. The neighbour was in bed, and at first refused to get up. But the man knocked and knocked; he knocked with shameless persistence; and at last the man in bed was forced to get up and give him what he needed. The second parable is the Parable of the Unjust Judge (Luke 18:2–7). It tells how there was a widow who wished for justice. In the same town there was an unjust judge. No one would ever have got a favourable verdict out of him without a handsome bribe, and the widow had no money. But she had one thing – she had persistence; and she kept coming back and back and back again, until the unjust judge gave her what she wanted for very weariness at her persistence. Often people take these parables to mean that, if we persist long enough in prayer, we will get what we want. If we batter at God's door long enough, if we badger God persistently enough, if we set up a bombardment and barrage of prayer, in the end God will succumb, and grant our request. That is not what these parables teach. A parable literally means *something which is laid alongside something else.* It comes from the two Greek words *para*, which means *beside*, and *ballein*, which means *to throw*. When we place two things alongside each other, we do so for the sake of comparison; but the point of the comparison may lie either in *resemblance* or in *contrast*. Many of Jesus' parables do work by resemblance, but these ones work by contrast. In these parables God is not *likened* to a churlish and unwilling householder or to an unjust and stubborn judge; he is *contrasted* with such a person. Jesus is saying: If a churlish and unwilling householder will in the end give a persistent friend the bread he needs, if an unjust and stubborn judge will in the end give a widow the justice for which she pleads, *how much more* will God, who is a loving father, give us what we need? That is the very thing which Jesus goes on to say. He bids us to ask that we may receive, to seek that we may find, to knock that it may be opened to us. If we, who are evil, know how to give good gifts to our children, *how much more* will our heavenly Father give us what is needful for life? (Luke 11:13; Matthew 7:11).

Here is the great and precious truth on which all prayer depends. God is not someone from whom gifts and favours have to be unwillingly extracted; he is not someone whose defences have to be battered down, and whose resistance has to be sapped and undermined. God is more willing to give than we are to ask.

> *Come, my soul, thy suit prepare;*
> *Jesus loves to answer prayer;*
> *He Himself has bid thee pray,*
> *Therefore will not say thee nay.*
>
> *Thou art coming to a King;*
> *Large petitions with thee bring;*
> *For His grace and power are such,*
> *None can ever ask too much.*

But we cannot leave this matter here, and it is because it is so often left here that so many people drift out of the habit of prayer. It is the basic truth of prayer that God is a loving father more ready to give than we are to ask. Does this mean that we have only to pray in order to receive, and that God will give us everything that we ask? That is precisely what it does not mean, and it is here that we must grasp and understand the laws of prayer.

The first law of prayer is that *we must be honest in prayer.* Luther said that the first law of prayer is, 'Don't lie to God.' The great temptation is to become conventional, to pray in pious language for the things for which we know we ought to pray. But the truth is that at least sometimes no one would be more shocked than we would be, if our prayer was granted. We may pray for the giving up of some habit – without the slightest intention of giving it up. We may pray for some virtue or quality – without any real desire to possess it. We may pray to be made into a certain kind of person – when the last thing that we in fact want is to be changed, and when we are very well content to be as we are. The peril of prayer is pious and unmeaning platitudes. The danger of prayer is that we very correctly ask for 'the right things', with no desire to receive them. That is lying to God. We cannot pray for that which we do not desire with our whole hearts. If there is something which we know we ought to desire, but do not, then our first step must be not to pray for it; that would be dishonest; but to confess that the holy desire which ought to be in our hearts is not there, and to ask God by his Spirit to put it there. There should be in our prayers an astringent honesty with ourselves, so that we may be honest with God, for God sees the secrets of our hearts, and well knows when we are conventionally asking for blessings which we have no real desire to receive.

A second law of prayer follows naturally from this; *we must be very definite in prayer.* It is not enough to ask God's forgiveness, because we are wretched and miserable sinners. That is far too easy and too comfortable. We must name and confess our actual sins to God. It is not enough vaguely to thank God for all his gifts. We must specifically name the gifts for which we are giving thanks. It is not enough nebulously to ask God to make us good. We must ask for the particular things in which we know that we are lacking, and which we know that we need. Herein lies the great difficulty of prayer. *There can be no real prayer without self-examination.* And self-examination is difficult, exhausting, and, above all, shaming and humiliating. Many of us spend life running away from ourselves rather than facing ourselves. One of the great reasons why our prayers are not what they should be is that so few people will face the stern discipline of self-examination in the presence of God on which prayer is based. Prayer and self-examination go hand in hand.

But we cannot stop even here. Suppose we do have perfect faith in God as a loving and a generous father; suppose we are honest in prayer; suppose we do achieve the discipline of self-examination and the consequent definiteness in prayer; will we then receive anything for which we ask? There are still more laws which govern prayer and which we must always remember.

We must remember that we are bound up in the bundle of life. We are not single, detached, isolated units, we are part of a fellowship, a society, a community, whether we like it or not. Anything that we do necessarily affects other people. We are therefore bound to see that *God cannot grant a selfish request*. It may well happen that, if our prayer is granted, then someone else in some way suffers. It may well happen that to give us what we desire would deprive someone else of what he or she should have. We so often pray as if no one mattered but ourselves, as if we were the centre of the universe, as if life and all that is in it ought to be organized and adjusted for our special benefit. No prayer which is forgetful of others can ever be answered as we wish it to be answered. Mankind is the family of God, and there can be no spoiled children, who get whatever they cry for, in God's family.

It is even more important to remember that *God always knows best*. Very often in our ignorance we pray for things which, if they were given to us, would not be to our ultimate and lasting good. It could not be otherwise. Because we are human beings the only thing which we can see is the present moment. We do not know what is going to happen a week, a day, an hour, even a moment ahead. We are like people who come into a cinema in the middle of a film; we have not seen the beginning; we do not know the end; and the happenings on the screen are a mystery to us. God alone sees all time, and, therefore, God alone knows what is good for us; and, for that very reason, God can often best answer our prayers by *not* giving us that for which we ask. There is nothing specially mysterious about this. It is a principle which we ourselves often observe with our own children. The child asks for something; we love the child, and our desire is for nothing but the child's happiness; and we know that if the child were to get what he is asking for it would not be good for him, and might even be a danger to him, and do him an injury. It is so with us and God. We do not need to be very old to be able to look back on life and to see that, if certain of our prayers had been granted, life would be infinitely poorer than it is today. The fact is that there is no such thing as unanswered prayer. It has been wisely said that God has three answers to our prayers. Sometimes God says, 'Yes!' Sometimes God says 'No!' Sometimes God says, 'Wait!' From even our own limited experience of life it must surely be easy to see that, if God granted all our prayers, it would be very far from being for our ultimate good, and that God must often give us the true answer to our prayers by withholding what we ask. At the end of the day we shall see that there is no such thing as unanswered prayer, for God in his wisdom sends us the answer, not which our ignorance desires, but which his love and knowledge know to be best.

There is a further inevitable law of prayer. *God will not do for us that which we can do for ourselves.* Prayer is not an easy way out to save us from trouble. Prayer is not a means of evading our own responsibilities and of escaping our own allotted toil. We may put this in another way. No sooner have we prayed than we must set out to make our own prayers come true; prayer is the cooperation of our effort with the grace of God. It is when we make our greatest effort that God sends his greatest answer. But, when we do make that effort, God sends his answer without fail. Suppose there is a student who has done little or none of the work required for an examination; suppose he has idled away his time, or has given in to things which are good enough in themselves, but which are not the things which he ought to have been doing; suppose that then on the morning of the examination he enters the examination hall, picks up the examination paper, and finds that he cannot answer the prescribed questions; then suppose that he bows his head and prays devoutly, 'O God, help me to pass this examination.' This is not a real prayer. To answer it would be to reward laziness and to approve time given to the wrong things. But, suppose this student to have worked faithfully; suppose him to have a nervous and self-distrustful temperament; suppose him to know his work, and yet to be from the nervous point of view a bad examinee; suppose him then to bow his head and to pray, 'O God, you know how hard I have worked; and you know how easily I get excited and nervous; calm me and keep me calm; and help me to do justice to myself and to the work that I have done.' That is a prayer which, if it is prayed in humble trust, can and will be answered. In prayer the enabling grace of

God comes to meet the earnest effort of man.

There is little point in praying to be enabled to overcome some temptation, and then flirting with that temptation, playing with fire, and putting oneself in the very position in which the temptation can exert all its fascination. There is little point in praying that God will convert the heathen, and then in refusing to give a pound a week to make it possible to bring the Gospel to the heathen. There is little point in praying that the sorrowing may be comforted and the lonely cheered, unless we ourselves set out to bring comfort and cheer to the sad and the neglected in our own sphere. There is little point in praying for our home and for our loved ones, and in going on being as selfish and inconsiderate as we have been. If we are ill, and we go to a doctor, the doctor will prescribe some medicine, some diet, some course of treatment, some method of exercise; and, unless we agree to make the necessary effort of will to carry out the doctor's instructions, we might as well never have consulted him. The doctor's knowledge and our obedient effort and self-discipline must cooperate towards our cure. It is the same with prayer. Prayer would be an evil rather than a blessing, if it were only a way of getting God to do what we ourselves will not make the effort to do. God does not do things for us; he enables us to do them for ourselves. God's word to Ezekiel was, 'Son of man, stand on thy feet and I will speak to thee' (Ezekiel 2:1). God answers the prayer of the man who is spiritually, mentally and physically stripped for action, but not the prayer of the man who regards life in terms of the armchair. Many of our prayers would be answered if we were prepared with God's help to make the effort to make them come true.

There is still another law of prayer which we must always remember. *Prayer moves within the natural laws which govern life.* When we think of it, this is a necessity. The characteristic of this world is that it is a dependable world; if the laws which govern it were erratically suspended, it would cease to be an order and become a chaos. Suppose a man were accidentally to fall from the fortieth-floor window of a New York skyscraper, a good and devout man and a firm believer in prayer; suppose him, as he passes the twentieth floor, to pray, 'O God, stop me falling.' That is a prayer which cannot be answered, because in that moment that man is in the grip of the law of gravity, and to suspend the law of gravity would be to put an end, not to his fall, but to the world in general.

A very important conclusion follows from this. Prayer does not normally promise or achieve release from some situation; it brings power and endurance to meet and to overcome that situation. In the Garden of Gethsemane Jesus prayed, if it was God's will, to be released from the Cross. He was not released from the Cross, but he was given power to endure the Cross.

Let us take a very simple example of this. It is sometimes the custom to pray for good weather for the day of a children's outing or the like. Such a prayer is quite wrong. It is not prayer but atmospheric conditions which determine the weather, and in any event the farmer may well be praying for rain for his parched crops. The correct prayer in such conditions is that we may be enabled to enjoy the day with glad cheerfulness, hail, rain or shine.

The basic mistake which so many people make about prayer is that almost instinctively they regard prayer as a means of escape from a situation; and prayer is not primarily a means of escape, it is a means of conquest. The laws of life are not relaxed for us by prayer, but through prayer there comes the strength and power to endure and to overcome any situation.

We must now step aside from these great laws and principles of prayer to look at the methods of prayer. There are five great divisions of prayer. There is *Invocation*. Invocation means *calling* or *inviting in*. But we must be clear what we mean by invocation. Invocation does not mean that we invite God to be present at our prayers, for God is everywhere and always present. It is far truer that in invocation we ask God to help us to realize that he is already with us, and to make us aware and conscious of his presence. God is not some distant stranger who has to be invited and persuaded into meeting with us; he is 'closer to us than breathing and nearer than hands and feet', as Tennyson said. There is an unwritten saying of Jesus, which is not in the gospels but which is very beautiful: 'Wherever there are two, they are not without God, and wherever there is one alone, I say I am with him. Raise the stone, and thou shalt find me; cleave the wood and there I am.' When the mason is working with the stone, or the carpenter with the wood, Jesus Christ is there. In invocation we remind ourselves that God is here.

There is *Confession*. In confession we tell God of our sins and our mistakes; we tell him that we are truly sorry for them; and we ask his forgiveness for them. Two things are necessary in confession, two things which go hand in hand. These are necessary searching self-examination and uncompromising honesty with ourselves. There is a kind of folly which seeks to hide things not only from our fellow men and women, but even from ourselves and from God. But God is the searcher of the hearts of men, the one who understands our thoughts afar off, the one from whom nothing is hidden or concealed. Maybe we ask: 'If God knows it all already, why should I have to tell him about it? If God loves me, and desires above all things to forgive me, why do I have to ask his forgiveness?' We must think in human terms, for they are the only terms in which we can think. When a child does something wrong, the parent knows it. The parent wants above all things to forgive, and the parent knows that the child is sorry for what he has done. But in spite of all that there is an unseen barrier between parent and child until the child comes of his own accord, and says, 'I'm sorry I was bad.' Then the barrier is down, and love is in the sunshine again. It is so with us and God. 'If we confess our sins, he is faithful and just to forgive us our sins, and to cleanse us from all unrighteousness' (I John 1:9). There is one thing still to add. Confession without amendment is a sadly truncated thing. We must use the forgiving love of God not as a comfortable excuse for sinning, but as an inescapable challenge and obligation to goodness. The child says, 'I'm sorry. I'll try to be better.' And we must say the same.

There is *Thanksgiving*. Thanksgiving is the outcome of the natural gratitude of the heart. There are three kinds of thanksgiving. There is the thanksgiving for Jesus Christ, God's greatest and best gift to humanity. There is the thanksgiving for all the means of grace and for all the great joys and wonders of life, and for all the gifts of God which have helped us to meet the great moments of life. But there is a third kind of thanksgiving. One of the great dangers of life is that we should take people or things for granted. In life there are people who have become part of our lives; they are woven into the structure of life. And the danger is that we should regard them as no more than part of the landscape, part of the essential background of life. There are gifts which come to us so regularly day by day that we forget that they are gifts. And there must be thanksgiving for these things. When we think of what life would be like without the people and the things which are part of everyday life, then the whole day is not long enough to give thanks for them to God.

There is *Petition*. Petition is that part of prayer in which we ask God for the things which we need for life and living. Petition is born of a sense of our own insufficiency and a realization of the all-sufficiency of God. Here again there is need for self-examination, because we must realize our own need of help and healing before we are able to ask for them. Especially in petition prayer is the greatest test and touchstone in the world. In petition we take our hopes and dreams and desires to God. Whenever a thing is laid in the presence of God, its true character is at once made clear. Sometimes when we lay something in the presence of God, we see its unimportance. It often happens that, when we lay before God something which was worrying us, or something on which we had set our heart, it falls into its proper proportion, and we see that it does not matter so much after all. Sometimes when we lay a thing before God, we see how impossible it is that we should ask for it, and how wrong it is that we should desire it. One of the greatest tests of anything is – Can I pray for it? Sometimes when we lay a thing before God, we see that indeed this is something on which we may truly set our hearts and towards which we may truly direct our efforts and our lives. In petition we take the needs of life and spread them before God.

In this too we may ask the question, If God already in his wisdom knows what is good for me, and if God already in his love is even more willing to give than I am to ask, why must I ask at all? Why should I not simply leave it to God to give? Once again we must think in human terms. We may know what is good for a child or a young person or a loved one. We may be willing to give it even at the price of sacrifice. But we cannot give it until it will be accepted; we cannot give it until it is asked; we cannot give it until they tell us that they wish to receive it. It is so with us and God. One of the great wonders about God is his respect for the rights of human personality. God does not force his gifts upon us. He waits for us to tell him that we are willing to receive them. And, therefore, in petition, we do not so much tell God what we want; rather we ask him to give what he wills, and what he knows is best.

There is *Intercession*. In intercession we take the needs of the world and bring them to God for his blessing and his help. We remember before God those in illness and in distress of mind and all those whom we know specially to need God's blessing. In particular in intercession we ask God's blessing and God's keeping for our nearest and our dearest. It will always bring us comfort and peace of mind to leave those whom we love in the strong hands of God.

We began at the very beginning by saying that prayer is the most natural activity in the world. Since that is so, prayer should be made perfectly naturally. There is no one right position in which to pray. It does not matter whether we kneel, or stand, or sit, or lie. There is only one necessity; we should be in a position in which we are not conscious of our bodies at all. Any bodily crampedness or discomfort takes our thoughts away from what we are doing. We must find for ourselves the position in which we most easily pray.

It is even more important to remember that there is no special language in which to pray. We do not need to use biblical or prayer-book language; we do not need to use 'Thou's and 'Thee's'. We can talk to God as easily and as naturally as we talk to our closest friend, because God is our closest friend. It is told that there was once a man who wished very much to pray, but he did not know how he ought to begin. A wise friend said to him: 'Sit down alone in your room. Put an empty chair opposite you. Imagine to yourself that Jesus is sitting in that chair. And talk to him as you would to the closest friend you have.' God is not looking for perfect English style, or even for perfect grammar. God is not caring whether or not we speak to him in perfectly phrased sentences. All that God wants is that we should speak to him. Formalities of position and formalities of language mean nothing to God. He wants us to feel at home in his presence, and to talk to him like a friend.

Because God is our friend, there is one thing we ought specially to remember about prayer. One of the sad things about our attitude to prayer is that so many of us connect prayer with the emergencies and the crises of life. When we are in trouble, when death and sorrow come, when there is illness and life is in danger, when there is worry and anxiety, when we are separated from those we love, then we pray. But when life is ordinary and things are going smoothly, when the sun is shining and the weather is calm, we forget to pray. When we act like that, it is as if we only remembered our best friend when we were in trouble and when we wanted to make use of him. It is inevitable that there will be times when prayer is more intense than at other times; but prayer should be for us a constant thing. 'A man, sir,' said Dr Johnson, 'should keep his friendship in constant repair.' Our friendship with God should be a daily and a constant thing. Bertram Pollock was at one time Bishop of Norwich; and the life of a bishop is a very busy life. In the memoir which she wrote of him his wife tells how every day in life he had certain hours set apart for prayer. No matter who came to see him at such times, he would say, 'Put him in an anteroom and tell him to wait. I have an appointment with God.' We should have our appointment each day with God; that engagement should be a priority engagement which nothing is allowed to break. There is something shameful in going to a friend only when we need him and when we want to get something out of him; and there is something shameful in treating God as someone to be made use of only when we are in trouble and when life goes wrong. In sunshine and in shadow we should have our times with God.

We have left the most important thing of all to the end. We have been speaking all the time so far as if prayer were always talking to God. But prayer is not a monologue in which we do all the talking; prayer is listening even more than it is talking. The highest form of prayer is silence when we wait on God and listen to God. We have a low view of prayer if we regard prayer as a way of telling God what we want him to do; prayer is even more listening to God, as he tells us what he wants us to do. Prayer is not a way of making use of God; prayer is a way of offering ourselves to God in order that he should be able to make use of us. It may be that one of our great faults in prayer is that we talk too much and listen too little. When prayer is at its highest we wait in silence for God's voice to speak to us; we linger in his presence for his peace and his power to flow over us and around us; we lean back in his everlasting arms and feel the serenity of perfect security in him.

If we remember these things, prayer will not be a grim duty or a dull routine or a conventional duty; it will be the greatest thing in life, for in its power we shall find that we will emerge triumphantly from anything that life can do to us.

This book is offered as a help to those who wish to pray. There are prayers for morning and evening in the family circle. And there are prayers, some of them much more personal, for the special occasions in life. Those who use this book will naturally wish to insert into these prayers their own prayers which rise from their own situation, and from their own needs and desires. And this book will have fulfilled its aim when those who use it discard it, and use it no longer, but speak to God in their own words, and in their own way.

I send out this book as a help for those who wish to pray within the family circle and for themselves. And it is my own prayer that those who use it will finally come not to need its help any more.

PRAYERS WITH
BIBLE READINGS FOR
SEVENTY DAYS

FIRST DAY

O God, our Father, who ever makes the light to shine out of the darkness, we thank you for waking us to see the light of this new day. Grant to us to waste none of its hours; to soil none of its moments; to neglect none of its opportunities; to fail in none of its duties. And bring us to the evening time undefeated by any temptation, at peace with ourselves, at peace with our fellow men and women, and at peace with you. This we ask for your love's sake. AMEN.

In the evening

O God, our Father, we thank you for this day which is passing from us now.

For any glimpse of beauty we have seen;
For any echo of your truth that we have heard;
For any kindness that we have received;
For any good that we have been enabled to do;
And for any temptation which you gave us grace to overcome:
We thank you, O God.

We ask your forgiveness for anything which has spoiled and marred this day.
For any word which now we wish that we had never spoken;
For any deed which now we wish that we had never done;
For everything which makes us ashamed when we remember it;
Forgive us, O God.

Eternal God, who gives us the day for work and the night for rest, grant us, as we go to rest, a good night's sleep; and wake us refreshed tomorrow, better able to serve you and to serve our fellow men and women. This we ask, through Jesus Christ our Lord. AMEN.

Matthew 5:1–12

And seeing the multitudes, he went up into a mountain: and when he was set, his disciples came unto him: And he opened his mouth, and taught them, saying, Blessed are the poor in spirit: for theirs is the kingdom of heaven. Blessed are they that mourn: for they shall be comforted. Blessed are the meek: for they shall inherit the earth. Blessed are they which do hunger and thirst after righteousness: for they shall be filled. Blessed are the merciful: for they shall obtain mercy. Blessed are the pure in heart: for they shall see God. Blessed are the peacemakeres: for they shall be called the children of God. Blessed are they which are persecuted for righteousness' sake: for theirs is the kingdom of heaven. Blessed are ye, when men shall revile you, and persecute you, and shall say all manner of evil against you falsely, for my sake. Rejoice, and be exceeding glad: for great is your reward in heaven: for so persecuted they the prophets which were before you.

SECOND DAY

IN THE MORNING

O God, our Father, bless us and keep us all through today.

At our work, make us diligent, ever showing ourselves to be workmen who have no need to be ashamed.

In our pleasure, help us to find delight only in such things as bring no regrets to follow.

In our homes, make us kind and considerate, ever trying to make the work of others easier, and not harder.

In our dealings with our fellow men and women, make us courteous and kindly.

In our dealings with ourselves, make us honest to face the truth.

And in every moment of this day make us ever to remember that you, God, see us, and that in you we live and move and have our being. So grant that we may do nothing which would bring shame to ourselves, grief to those who love us, and sorrow to you: through Jesus Christ our Lord.   AMEN.

IN THE EVENING

O God, our Father, who has bidden us to pray for all people, we remember at evening time those who specially need our prayers.

Bless those who are lonely, and who feel their loneliness worst of all at evening time.

Bless those who are sad, and who at evening feel most of all the absence of someone whom they loved, and lost awhile.

Bless those who are ill, and who will not sleep this night; and those who this night will wake to ease the sufferer's pain.

Bless those who have no home, and no family circle to call their own.

O God, who are everywhere present, bless this our home, and help us to remember that Jesus is always our unseen guest, and so help us never in this place to do or to say anything which would make Him sad to see.

Keep us this night in the dark hours, and grant us kindly sleep, and make us to feel around us and about us the clasp of the everlasting arms, which will never let us go: through Jesus Christ our Lord. AMEN.

DAILY READING

Psalm 145:9–16

The Lord is good to all: and his tender mercies are all over his works.

All thy works shall praise thee, O Lord; and thy saints shall bless thee.

They shall speak of the glory of thy kingdom, and talk of thy power;

To make known to the sons of men his mighty acts, and the glorious majesty of his kingdom.

Thy kingdom is an everlasting kingdom, and thy dominion endureth throughout all generations.

The Lord upholdeth all that fall, and raiseth up all those that be bowed down.

The eyes of all wait upon thee; and thou givest them their meat in due season.

Thou openest thine hand, and satisfiest the desire of every living thing.

THIRD DAY

O God, our Father, who has bidden us to live in fellowship with
one another, keep us from everything which would make us
difficult to live with today.

Help us never thoughtlessly or deliberately to speak in such a way
that we would hurt another's feelings, or wound another's
heart.

Keep us from all impatience, from all irritability, and from a temper
which is too quick.
Keep us from eyes which are focused to find fault and from a
tongue which is tuned to criticize.
Keep us from being touchy, and quick to take offence, and slow
to forget it.
Help us not to be stubborn and obstinate, and keep us from the
selfishness which can see nothing but its own point of view,
and which wants nothing but its own way.

Grant to us all through this day something of the grace and beauty
which shone upon our blessed Lord.

Hear this our prayer, for your love's sake.   AMEN.

In the evening

Eternal God, who gave us this day, and who now at evening time
are taking it back to yourself, forgive us for all which we did
not do today.

Forgive us for any word of comfort, of praise, of thanks, which
we might have spoken, and did not speak.
Forgive us for any help we might have given to someone in need,
and did not give.

Forgive us if today we have made things more difficult for anyone.

Forgive us if by word or action we have set a bad example to anyone, and have made it easier for another to go wrong.

Forgive us if today we have been disloyal to any friend, or if we have hurt the hearts of those whom above all we ought to cherish.

Grant us this night your gift of sleep; and grant us grace that tomorrow we may walk more closely to you: through Jesus Christ our Lord. AMEN.

DAILY READING

Luke 12:15–21

And he said unto them, Take heed, and beware of covetousness: for a man's life consisteth not in the abundance of the things which he possesseth. And he spake a parable unto them, saying, The ground of a certain rich man brought forth plentifully: and he thought within himself, saying, What shall I do, because I have no room where to bestow my fruits? And he said, This will I do: I will pull down my barns, and build greater; and there will I bestow all my fruits and my goods. And I will say to my soul, Soul, thou hast much goods laid up for many years; take thine ease, eat, drink, and be merry. But God said unto him, Thou fool, this night thy soul shall be required of thee: then whose shall those things be, which thou hast provided? So is he that layeth up treasure for himself, and is not rich toward God.

FOURTH DAY

O God, our Creator and our Father, who has given to us the gift
of life, bless us this day as we go to the work which has been
given us to do.

We give you thanks for our work, and for the health to do it.
We thank you for skill of hand, for accuracy of eye and mind and
brain, to earn a living and to do the work of a house and home.
We thank you for the friends and the comrades whom you have
given to us, for those in whose company joys are doubly dear,
and in whose presence sorrow's pain is soothed.

Help us today to be so cheerful, that it may make others happier
to meet us.
Help us to be so true to you, that we may be a strength to others
who are tempted.

O Lord Jesus, we have begun the day with you; grant that your
reflection may be upon us throughout all its hours. This we ask
for your love's sake.   AMEN.

IN THE EVENING

O God, the Giver of every good gift, there is so much for which
we ought to give you thanks.

We thank you for going out in the morning, and for coming home
at evening time.
We thank you for the joy of work, and for all clean pleasures which
rest our body and relax our mind.
We thank you for the light of the morning, and for the dark of
the night.
We thank you for the day with all its duties and its tasks, and for
the night and kindly sleep.

Grant us this night a mind at rest.

Grant that we may forget our worries in the peace that passes understanding; and that we may lose our anxieties in the certainty that neither we nor those we love can drift beyond your love and care.

Grant to us to sleep in peace and to wake in strength, because we sleep and wake in you; through Jesus Christ our Lord. AMEN.

DAILY READING

Matthew 5:13–16

Ye are the salt of the earth: but if the salt have lost his savour, wherewith shall it be salted? it is thenceforth good for nothing, but to be cast out, and to be trodden under foot of men. Ye are the light of the world. A city that is set on an hill cannot be hid. Neither do men light a candle, and put it under a bushel, but on a candelstick; and it giveth light unto all that are in the house. Let your light so shine before men, that they may see your good works, and glorify your Father which is in heaven.

FIFTH DAY

Eternal and everblessed God, who are the Lord of all good life, we do not know what will come to us and what will happen to us today. Whatever comes to us, be with us to guide and to strengthen, to comfort and control.

If temptation comes to us, give us grace to overcome evil and to do the right.

If we have to make important decisions, give us grace ever to choose the right way, and to refuse the wrong way.

If it will be difficult to witness for you, give us courage never to be ashamed to show whose we are and whom we serve.

If things go well with us, keep us from all pride, and keep us from thinking that we do not need you.

If we shall know sorrow, failure, disappointment, loss, keep us from all despair, and help us never to give in.

O you who are the Light of the World, be with us today, whatever light may shine or shadow fall, that we may ever live and walk as children of the light: through Jesus Christ our Lord.   AMEN.

In the evening

O God, our Father, who has given us a life to live, and a task to do, bless us at eventide.

Forgive us for the things which we have left half done today, and for the things which we have not even begun.

Forgive us for the plans that we made, and did not carry out; and for the dreams which are still only dreams.

Forgive us for the promises which we made to you and to our fellow men and women, and did not keep.

O God, our Father, bless those who this night specially need your blessing.

Bless those on journeys by sea and land and air; those who this night will lie down in hunger and in cold; those who are in prison and in disgrace; those who are ill and who will not sleep tonight; those who are sad and for whom the slow, dark hours are very lonely.

Bless each one of us, and be with us through this night, and stay with us until the day shall break and all the shadows flee away: through Jesus Christ our Lord. AMEN.

DAILY READING

Psalm 23

The Lord is my shepherd; I shall not want.
He maketh me to lie down in green pastures: he leadeth me beside the still waters.
He restoreth my soul: he leadeth me in the paths of righteousness for his name's sake.
Yea, though I walk through the valley of the shadow of death, I will fear no evil: for thou art with me; thy rod and thy staff they comfort me.
Thou preparest a table before me in the presence of mine enemies: thou anointest my head with oil; my cup runneth over.
Surely goodness and mercy shall follow me all the days of my life: and I will dwell in the house of the LORD for ever.

SIXTH DAY

O God, our Father, who has bidden us to be lights in this dark world, help us throughout all this day to be a help and an example to all whom we meet.

Help us to bring comfort to those in sorrow, and strength to those who are tempted.
Help us to bring courage to those who are afraid, and guidance to those who do not know what to do.
Help us to bring cheer to those who are discouraged, and encouragement to those who are depressed.

And grant that, as we move among men and women this day, they may catch a glimpse in us of the Master, whose we are and whom we seek to serve. This we ask for your love's sake. AMEN.

Eternal and everblessed God, we give you thanks, as this day comes to an end, for those who mean so much to us, and without whom life could never be the same.

We thank you for those to whom we can go at any time, and never feel a nuisance.
We thank you for those to whom we can go when we are tired, knowing that they have, for weary feet, the gift of rest.
We thank you for those with whom we can talk, and keep nothing back, knowing that they will not laugh at our dreams or mock at our failures.
We thank you for those in whose presence it is easier to be good.
We thank you for those in whose company joys are doubly dear, and sorrow's bitterness is soothed.

We thank you for those who by their warning, their counsel, and their rebuke have kept us from mistakes we might have made, and sins we might have committed.

And above all we thank you for Jesus, the pattern of our lives, the Lord of our hearts, and the Saviour of our souls.

Accept this our thanksgiving, and grant us tonight a good night's rest: through Jesus Christ our Lord.   AMEN.

DAILY READING

Psalm 121

I will lift up mine eyes unto the hills, from whence cometh my help.

My help cometh from the Lord, which made heaven and earth.

He will not suffer thy foot to be moved: he that keepeth thee will not slumber.

Behold, he that keepeth Israel shall neither slumber nor sleep.

The Lord is thy keeper: the Lord is thy shade upon thy right hand.

The sun shall not smite thee by day, nor the moon by night.

The Lord shall preserve thee from all evil: he shall preserve thy soul.

The Lord shall preserve thy going out and thy coming in from this time forth, and even for evermore.

SEVENTH DAY

In the morning

O God, our Father, who desires us to love and to serve one another, and who has created us for fellowship with you and with our fellow men and women, grant to us all through this day the gifts and the graces which will make us easy to live with.

Grant us courtesy, that we may live every moment as if we were living at the court of the King.

Grant us tolerance, that we may not be so quick to condemn what we do not like and what we do not understand.

Grant us considerateness, that we may think of the feelings of others even more than of our own.

Grant us kindliness, that we may miss no opportunity to help, to cheer, to comfort and to encourage a brother or sister.

Grant us honesty, that our work may be our best, whether there is anyone to see it or not.

Grant us so to live this day that the world may be a happier place because we passed through it; through Jesus Christ our Lord. AMEN.

In the evening

O God, our Father, we thank you that you 'didst keep us this day in our going out and in our coming in'.

We thank you that you enabled us to do our work, and that you kept us in safety on our journey to our work, and on the busy city streets.

We thank you for things to do, for friends to meet, and for all good pleasures to enjoy.

We thank you for clothes to wear, for food to eat, for a home from which we go out and to which at evening time we return, and for loved ones who ever care for us and take thought for all things for our comfort.

Grant that we may never take for granted all the things which come to us so regularly each day, but that we may ever remember you, the Giver of every good and perfect gift.

So grant to us this night to lay ourselves down in gratitude, and tomorrow to wake in resolution to serve you better for all your love to us: through Jesus Christ our Lord.   AMEN.

DAILY READING

Matthew 6:9–15

After this manner therefore pray ye: Our Father which art in heaven, Hallowed be thy name. Thy kingdom come. Thy will be done in earth, as it is in heaven. Give us this day our daily bread. And forgive us our debts, as we forgive our debtors. And lead us not into temptation, but deliver us from evil: For thine is the kingdom, and the power, and the glory, for ever. Amen.

For if ye forgive men their trespasses, your heavenly Father will also forgive you: but if ye forgive not men their trespasses, neither will your Father forgive your trespasses.

EIGHTH DAY

IN THE MORNING

O God, our Father, before we go out on the duties and the tasks of this day, we ask you to direct, to control, and to guide us all through its hours.

Grant that today we may never for one moment forget your presence.

Grant that we may take no step, and that we may come to no decision, without your guidance, and that, before we act, we may ever seek to find your will for us.

Be on our lips, that we may speak no evil word.

Be in our eyes, that they may never linger on any forbidden thing.

Be on our hands, that we may do our own work with diligence, and serve the needs of others with eagerness.

Be in our minds, that no soiled or bitter thought may gain an entry to them.

Be in our hearts, that they may be warm with love for Thee, and for our fellow men and women.

Help us to begin, to continue, and to end this day in you: through Jesus Christ our Lord.   AMEN.

IN THE EVENING

Eternal and everblessed God, help us this night to lay ourselves down in peace.

Give us that peace of mind which comes from casting all our burdens upon you, and from leaving ourselves and our loved ones entirely to your care.

Give us that peace which comes from being in perfect personal relationships with our fellow men and women, with no misunderstandings between us and them, and with no bitterness to anyone.

Give us the peace of sins forgiven, which comes from the certainty
that, through Jesus Christ, there is no barrier between ourselves
and you.

And, above all, give us the peace of your presence, and the
certainty that in light and in dark you will never leave us, nor
forsake us, and that you will never let us go: through Jesus
Christ our Lord.   AMEN.

DAILY READING

Psalm 43

Judge me, O God, and plead my cause against an ungodly nation:
O deliver me from the deceitful and unjust man.
For thou art the God of my strength: why dost thou cast me off?
why go I mourning because of the oppression of the enemy?
O send out thy light and thy truth: let them lead me; let them
bring me unto thy holy hill, and to thy tabernacles.
Then will I go unto the altar of God, unto God my exceeding joy:
yea, upon the harp will I praise thee, O God my God.
Why are thou cast down, O my soul? and why art thou disquieted
within me? hope in God: for I shall yet praise him, who is the
health of my countenance, and my God.

NINTH DAY

In the morning

O God, our Father, help us all through this day so to live that we
    may bring help to others, credit to ourselves and to the name
    we bear, and joy to those who love us, and to you.

Help us to be
    Cheerful when things go wrong;
    Persevering when things are difficult;
    Serene when things are irritating.

Enable us to be
    Helpful to those in difficulties;
    Kind to those in need;
    Sympathetic to those whose hearts are sore and sad.

Grant that
    Nothing may make us lose our temper;
    Nothing may take away our joy;
    Nothing may ruffle our peace;
    Nothing may make us bitter towards any man.

So grant that all through this day all with whom we work, and
    all whom we meet, may see in us the reflection of the Master,
    whose we are, and whom we seek to serve. This we ask for your
    love's sake.   AMEN.

In the evening

Eternal God, this night we thank you for your good hand upon
    us through all this day.
We thank you that you have enabled us to do our work, and to
    earn a living for ourselves and for those we love.
We thank you for the voice within us which spoke to us when
    we were tempted to do wrong, and for the grace which kept
    us right.

We thank you for your protecting power, which has brought us in safety to this evening hour.

O God, with whom is forgiveness, forgive us, if today we have failed a friend, hurt a loved one, shamed ourselves, and grieved you.
Forgive us if we have been slack in duty to our fellow men and women, or careless in remembering you.

And now grant to us to sleep in peace, and to wake in strength: through Jesus Christ our Lord.   AMEN.

DAILY READING

Matthew 9:10–13

And it came to pass, as Jesus sat at meat in the house, behold, many publicans and sinners came and sat down with him and his disciples. And when the Pharisees saw it, they said unto his disciples, Why eateth your Master with publicans and sinners? But when Jesus heard that, he said unto them, They that be whole need not a physician, but they that are sick. But go ye and learn what that meaneth, I will have mercy and not sacrifice: for I am not come to call the righteous, but sinners to repentance.

TENTH DAY

IN THE MORNING

O God, our Father, save us this day from all the sins into which
we so easily and so continually fall.

Save us from demanding standards from others which we never
even try to satisfy ourselves.
Save us from being very easy on ourselves and very hard on others.
Save us from making excuses for things in ourselves which in
others we would condemn.
Save us from being wide-open-eyed to the faults of others, and
blind to our own.
Save us from taking for granted all that our loved ones do for us,
and from never realizing how much they do and how much
we demand.

Help us all through this day to try to do to others what we would
wish them to do to us, and so help us to fulfil the law of Jesus
Christ. This we ask for your love's sake.   AMEN.

IN THE EVENING

O God, our Father, this night we thank you for the comfort and
the companionship and the love of this our home.

We thank you for the joy of being together in a family.
We thank you for this day's work, and for this night's rest.

We ask you to bless those for whom there will be no sleep tonight;
those who must work throughout the night; those who journey
through the night by sea or land or air, to bring us our food,
our letters, and our newspapers for the morning; those who
must be on duty all night to maintain the public services, and
to ensure the safety and the security of others; doctors who
must wake to usher new life into the world, to close the eyes

---

of those for whom this life is passing away, to ease the sufferer's pain; nurses and all who watch by the bedside of those who are ill; those who this night will not sleep because of the pain of their body or the distress of their mind; those in misfortune, who will lie down in hunger and in cold.

Grant that in our own happiness and our own comfort we may never forget the sorrow and the pain, the loneliness and the need of others in the slow, dark hours. This we ask for your love's sake. AMEN.

DAILY READING

Isaiah 53:3–6

He is despised and rejected of men; a man of sorrows, and acquainted with grief: and we hid as it were our faces from him; he was despised, and we esteemed him not. Surely he hath borne our griefs, and carried our sorrows: yet we did esteem him stricken, smitten of God, and afflicted. But he was wounded for our transgressions, he was bruised for our iniquities; the chastisement of our peace was upon him; and with his stripes we are healed. All we like sheep have gone astray; we have turned every one to his own way; and the Lord hath laid on him the iniquity of us all.

ELEVENTH DAY

O God, our Father, grant us all through this day patience with things and patience with people.

If any task will be difficult, grant us the perseverance which will not admit defeat.
If any problem will be hard to solve, help us not to abandon it until we have found the solution.
If things will not come right the first time, help us to try and to try again, until failure becomes success.

Help us all through today never to lose our temper with people, however unfair, unjust, annoying and unpleasant they may be.
Help us to have time to listen to anyone who wants to talk to us about a worry, a problem, or a need.
Help us to be patient with those who are slow to learn and slow to understand.

Help us all through this day to work as Jesus worked, and to love as Jesus loved. This we ask for your love's sake. AMEN.

O God, our Father: as we look back across this day, we ask you to forgive us if today we have made things harder for others.

Forgive us if we have made work harder for others, by being careless, thoughtless, selfish and inconsiderate.
Forgive us if we have made faith harder for others, by laughing at things they hold precious, or casting doubts on things they hold dear.
Forgive us if we have made goodness harder for others, by setting them an example which would make it easier for them to go wrong.

Forgive us if we have made joy harder for others, by bringing gloom and depression through our grumbling discontent.

Forgive us, O God, for all the ugliness of our lives; and tomorrow help us to walk more nearly as our Master walked, that something of his grace and beauty may be on us. This we ask for your love's sake. AMEN.

DAILY READING

Romans 8:35–9

Who shall separate us from the love of Christ? shall tribulation, or distress, or persecution, or famine, or nakedness, or peril, or sword? As it is written, For thy sake we are killed all the day long; we are accounted as sheep for the slaughter. Nay, in all these things we are more than conquerors through him that loved us. For I am persuaded, that neither death, nor life, nor angels, nor principalities, nor powers, nor things present, nor things to come, Nor height, nor depth, nor any other creature, shall be able to separate us from the love of God, which is in Christ Jesus our Lord.

TWELFTH DAY

IN THE MORNING

O Lord our God, in whom we live and move and have our being, help us never to forget that you are beside us all through this day.

O Lord Jesus, who has promised that you are with us always, help us never to forget your presence all this day.

So grant that all this day every word we speak may be fit for you to hear; that every deed we do may be fit for you to see; that even every thought of our mind and every emotion of our heart may be fit to bear your scrutiny.

Grant that every task we do may be so well done that we can take it and show it to you.

Grant that every pleasure in which we share may be so honourable and so clean that we can ask you to share it with us.

So bring us to the evening time with nothing left undone, and nothing badly done; with nothing to regret and nothing to make us ashamed: through Jesus Christ our Lord. AMEN.

IN THE EVENING

O God, our Father, Master of all good workmen, always at evening time we remember the things which we have left undone.

Forgive us for the plans we made and did not carry out.
Forgive us for the resolutions we took and did not keep.
Forgive us for the promises we made and broke.
Forgive us for the tasks we began and never finished.

Grant that we may never put off a task or delay a decision until tomorrow, when it should be done and taken today. So help us to live that, whenever your call comes for us, at morning, at midday, or at evening, it may find us ready.

Now grant to us this night the sleep which will bring rest to our bodies and peace to our minds; and grant that we may rise tomorrow to be better workers and better servants of our Lord. This we ask for your love's sake.   AMEN.

DAILY READING

Psalm 95:1–7

O come, let us sing unto the Lord: let us make a joyful noise to the rock of our salvation.

Let us come before his presence with thanksgiving, and make a joyful noise unto him with psalms.

For the Lord is a great God, and a great King above all gods.

In his hand are the deep places of the earth: the strength of the hills is his also.

The sea is his, and he made it: and his hands formed the dry land.

O come, let us worship and bow down: let us kneel before the Lord our maker.

For he is our God; and we are the people of his pasture, and the sheep of his hand.

THIRTEENTH DAY

IN THE MORNING

Eternal God, who has given us the gift of this another day, help us to use wisely and to use well the time which you have given us.

Help us not to waste time on the wrong things, and on the things which do not matter.
Help us not to spend time in idleness, so that the hours go back to you unused and useless.
Help us not to put off until tomorrow that which should be done today, and ever to remember that we cannot tell if for us tomorrow will ever come.

Help us to do with our might each thing which our hand finds to do, and to do it as for you, that we may come to the evening time with nothing left undone, and nothing badly done: through Jesus Christ our Lord.   AMEN.

IN THE EVENING

O God, our Father, we thank you for all happy things which came to us this day.

We thank you for any kindness which we have received.
We thank you for any word of thanks or praise or encouragement which has come to us.
We thank you for anything which made us feel that we were needed and valued and appreciated.
We thank you for any new friendship that we have made, and for any old friendship which has become still more strong and precious.
We thank you for any temptation which we have been enabled to resist, and for any service that we have been enabled to render.

Accept, O God, all in this day which has been in accordance with your will, and forgive that which has not been so; and help us to lay ourselves to sleep in perfect fellowship with you and with our fellow men and women: through Jesus Christ our Lord. AMEN.

DAILY READING

Ephesians 6:11–18

Put on the whole armour of God, that ye may be able to stand against the wiles of the devil. For we wrestle not against flesh and blood, but against principalities, against powers, against the rulers of the darkness of this world, against spiritual wickedness in high places. Wherefore take unto you the whole armour of God, that ye may be able to withstand in the evil day, and having done all, to stand. Stand therefore, having your loins girt about with truth, and having on the breastplate of righteousness; And your feet shod with the preparation of the gospel of peace; Above all taking the shield of faith, wherewith ye shall be able to quench all the fiery darts of the wicked. And take the helmet of salvation, and the sword of the Spirit, which is the word of God: Praying always with all prayer and supplication in the Spirit, and watching thereunto with all perseverance and supplication for all saints.

FOURTEENTH DAY

─────────

O God, our Father, save us from these thoughts and feelings which
only succeed in making life wretched and unhappy for
ourselves and for others.

Save us from foolish discontent, and help us at all times to do
the best we can with the resources we have.
Save us from the envy which forgets to count its own blessings,
because it thinks so much of those of others.
Save us from the jealousy which grudges others every gift and
every success.
Save us from vain regrets about things which cannot be altered;
and give us grace to accept the situation in which we are, and
there to serve you with your whole heart.
Save us from the bitterness which poisons life for ourselves and
for others.

So grant that, cleansed from self and cleansed from sin, our lives
may bring joy to others and contentment to ourselves: through
Jesus Christ our Lord.   AMEN.

O God, our Father, bless those who at the day's ending specially
need your blessing.

Bless those who are far from home and far from friends, and who
are lonely as the shadows fall.
Bless those who have made mistakes and who are sorry now.
Bless those who are sad, and for whom loneliness is most lonely
at evening time.
Bless those who are in illness and in pain, and for whom the night
is slow and long.

─────────

Bless the people with whom we work every day.

Bless all our friends, and keep them true to us, and us true to them.

Bless our loved ones, and let nothing ever come between us and them.

Bless this family, and grant that it may be true of this home that, where two or three are gathered together you are there in the midst of them.

Bless each one of us. You know our needs better than we know them ourselves. Open your hand and satisfy them all: through Jesus Christ our Lord. AMEN.

DAILY READING

Psalm 119:97–104

O how love I thy law! it is my meditation all the day.

Thou through thy commandments hast made me wiser than mine enemies: for they are ever with me.

I have more understanding than all my teachers: for thy testimonies are my meditation.

I understand more than the ancients, because I keep thy precepts.

I have refrained my feet from every evil way, that I might keep thy word.

I have not departed from thy judgements: for thou hast taught me.

How sweet are thy words unto my taste! yea, sweeter than honey to my mouth!

Through thy precepts I get understanding: therefore I hate every false way.

FIFTEENTH DAY

IN THE MORNING

Eternal God, grant that we may count it a day wasted when we do not learn something new, and when we are not a little further on the way to goodness and to you.

Help us to try to do our work better every day.
Help us to try to add something to our store of knowledge every day.
Help us to try to know someone better every day.

Grant to us each day to learn more of self-mastery and self-control.
Grant to us each day better to rule our temper and our tongue.
Grant to us each day to leave our faults farther behind and to grow more nearly into the likeness of our Lord.

So grant that at the end of this day, and at the end of every day, we may be nearer to you than when the day began: through Jesus Christ our Lord.   AMEN.

IN THE EVENING

O God, our Father, forgive us for the failures of today.

Forgive us for any failure in self-control, through which we said or did things for which we are sorry now.
Forgive us for any failure in self-discipline, through which we were slack, when we should have been doing with our might that which our hand found to do.
Forgive us for any failure in obedience, through which we listened to our own desires rather than to your will.

We give you thanks for anything of good that has been in this day.

We thank you for any temptation which you enabled us to overcome.

We thank you for any help you enabled us to give, and for any
   service you enabled us to render.
We thank you for any good word which you enabled us to speak,
   and any good deed which you enabled us to do.

So now we render this day back to you, with all its dark times
   and all its shining moments, that you may accept its goodness
   and forgive its sin: through Jesus Christ our Lord.   AMEN.

DAILY READING

Matthew 20:25–8

Jesus called them unto him, and said, Ye know that the princes
of the Gentiles exercise dominion over them, and they that are
great exercise authority upon them. But it shall not be so among
you: but whosoever will be great among you, let him be your
minister; And whosoever will be chief among you, let him be your
servant: Even as the Son of man came not to be ministered unto,
but to minister, and to give his life a ransom for many.

SIXTEENTH DAY

O God, our Father, we are ashamed when we remember how so often we hurt most of all those whom we ought to cherish most of all, and how we treat our nearest and dearest in a way in which we would never dare to behave towards strangers. Grant that it may not be so today.

Take from us the carelessness, the selfishness, the inconsiderateness, the untidiness, which make the work of others harder than it ought to be.
Take from us the lack of sensitiveness which makes us hurt the feelings of others and never even realize that we are doing so.
Take from us the habit of unkind criticism and of nagging fault-finding, the temper of crossness and irritability, which wreck the peace of any home.
Take from us the disobedience which brings anxiety, and the disloyalty which brings sorrow to those who love us.

Grant that all through today we may so speak and so act that we will bring nothing but happiness to those whose love is our privilege, and whose friendship is our joy: through Jesus Christ our Lord. AMEN.

IN THE EVENING

O God, our Father, we thank you for everything which has happened to us today, because we know that in it and through it all you have been loving us with an everlasting love.

We thank you alike for sorrow and for joy, for laughter and for tears, for silence and for song.
We thank you for any success to lift life up, and for any failure to keep us humble and to help us not to forget our need of you.

We thank you for joys which will be to us for ever and for ever happy memories, and we thank you for sorrows which made us go to you because we had nowhere else to go.

Grant us at all times, no matter what is happening to us, the certainty that you are working all things together for good. And so grant that this night our pillow may be peace: through Jesus Christ our Lord.   AMEN.

DAILY READING

Psalm 103:8–13

The Lord is merciful and gracious, slow to anger, and plenteous in mercy.

He will not always chide: neither will he keep his anger for ever.

He hath not dealt with us after our sins; nor rewarded us according to our iniquities.

For as the heaven is high above the earth, so great is his mercy toward them that fear him.

As far as the east is from the west, so far hath he removed our transgressions from us.

Like as a father pitieth his children, so the Lord pitieth them that fear him.

SEVENTEENTH DAY

O God, our Father, help us to walk with wisdom all this day.

Help us never to flirt with temptation, and never to play with fire.
Help us never needlessly or thoughtlessly to put ourselves into
a position in which temptation has the opportunity to exert its
power over us.
Help us never to allow our eyes to linger, or our thoughts to dwell,
on the forbidden things, lest their fascination be too strong for
our resistence.

Help us to walk every step of today looking ever unto Jesus, that
his light may be our guide, that his presence may be our
defence, and that his love may be our strength and inspiration.
This we ask for your love's sake. AMEN.

O God, our Father, giver of every good and perfect gift, put into
our hearts gratitude for all that you have done for us today.

Help us not to forget that today you have kept us in our going out
and our coming in, and have brought us to this evening hour;
that today you have fed us and clothed us and given us life and
kept us alive; that today you have preserved us in body, mind
and spirit, and hast surrounded us with love both human and
divine.
O God, our Father, who always accepts the offering of the humble
and the contrite heart, put into our hearts penitence for all the
failures, the faults, the mistakes, the sins of this day. Make us
see ourselves and our sins in the light of your pure
countenance. So make us truly sorry for every wrong thing
which has shamed ourselves and grieved you, and then grant

us, before we sleep, your kiss of pardon and of peace: through Jesus Christ our Lord.   AMEN.

Luke 15:3–10

And he spake this parable unto them, saying, What man of you, having an hundred sheep, if he lose one of them, doth not leave the ninety and nine in the wilderness, and go after that which is lost, until he find it? And when he hath found it, he layeth it on his shoulders, rejoicing. And when he cometh home, he calleth together his friends and neighbours, saying unto them, Rejoice with me; for I have found my sheep which was lost. I say unto you, that likewise joy shall be in heaven over one sinner that repenteth, more than over ninety and nine just persons, which need no repentance. Either what woman having ten pieces of silver, if she lose one piece, doth not light a candle, and sweep the house, and seek diligently till she find it? And when she hath found it, she calleth her friends and her neighbours together, saying, Rejoice with me; for I have found the piece which I had lost. Likewise, I say unto you, there is joy in the presence of the angels of God over one sinner that repenteth.

EIGHTEENTH DAY

IN THE MORNING

O God, our Father, we know that every day comes to us from you filled with new opportunities; and we know that today will be like that.

We know that today will bring us the opportunity to do some useful work, and to justify our existence in the world; help us to do that work with all our might.

We know that today will bring us the opportunity to learn something new, and to add something to the store of our knowledge; help us to seize that opportunity.

We know that today will bring us the opportunity to witness for you, and to show on whose side we are; help us fearlessly to bear that witness.

We know that today will bring us an opportunity to lend a helping hand to those whose need is greater than our own; help us to be among our fellow men and women as they who serve.

We know that today will bring us the opportunity to come closer to each other and nearer to you; grant that we may so take that opportunity that, when the evening comes, we may be bound more firmly in comradeship to one another, and in love to you: through Jesus Christ our Lord. AMEN.

IN THE EVENING

O God, our Father, forgive us if we have been too lazy today.

Forgive us if we have left undone tasks which should have been done; if we have left untaken decisions which should have been taken; if we have not kept the promises we should have kept.

O God, our Father, forgive us if we have allowed ourselves to be too busy today.

Forgive us if we have been too busy to help a friend, even if it was only by patiently listening to his troubles; if we have been too busy to fulfil our duties to our family and to our home. Forgive us if moment has added itself to moment, and hour to hour, and we were too busy to think of you.

Grant to us this night to sleep well, and, in the morning, grant to us to wake and to work without haste and without rest, so that, like our Master, we may finish the work which you have given us to do. This we ask for your love's sake. AMEN.

DAILY READING

Psalm 19:7–11

The law of the Lord is perfect, converting the soul: the testimony of the Lord is sure, making wise the simple.

The statutes of the Lord are right, rejoicing the heart: the commandment of the Lord is pure, enlightening the eyes.

The fear of the Lord is clean, enduring for ever: the judgements of the Lord are true and righteous altogether.

More to be desired are they than gold, yea, than much fine gold: sweeter also than honey and the honeycomb.

Moreover by them is thy servant warned: and in keeping of them there is great reward.

NINETEENTH DAY

O God, our Father, deliver us this day from all that would keep us from serving you and from serving our fellow men and women as we ought.

Deliver us from all coldness of heart; and grant that neither our hand nor our heart may ever remain shut to the appeal of someone's need.

Deliver us from all weakness of will; from the indecision which cannot make up its mind; from the irresolution which cannot abide by a decision once it is made; from the inability to say No to the tempting voices which come to us from inside and from outside.

Deliver us from all failure in endeavour; from being too easily discouraged; from giving up and giving in too soon; from allowing any task to defeat us because it is difficult.

Grant us this day the love which is generous in help; the determination which is steadfast in decision; the perseverance which is enduring to the end; through Jesus Christ our Lord.

AMEN.

IN THE EVENING

O God, our Father, take from our minds this night the worries and anxieties which would keep us from sleeping. Help us to make up our minds bravely to deal with the things which can be dealt with, and not to worry about the things which we can do nothing.

Take from our hearts this night the feelings which would keep us from resting; take from us all discontent, all envy and jealousy, all vain and useless longings for the things which are not for us.

Take from our bodies the tension which would keep us from relaxing; and help us to lean back in the clasp of the everlasting arms.

Into your hands we commit our loved ones, knowing that, even if they are absent from us, they are for ever present with you. Into your hands we commit ourselves that in your keeping, in light and in dark, in life and in death, we may be safe.

Hear these our prayers, through Jesus Christ our Lord.   AMEN.

DAILY READING

Mark 10:13–16

And they brought young children to him, that he should touch them: and his disciples rebuked those that brought them. But when Jesus saw it, he was much displeased, and said unto them, Suffer the little children to come unto me, and forbid them not: for of such is the kingdom of God. Verily I say unto you, Whosoever shall not receive the kingdom of God as a little child, he shall not enter therein. And he took them up in his arms, put his hands upon them, and blessed them.

TWENTIETH DAY

O God, our Father, who has given us the rest of the night, and who now sends us forth to the work of the day, guide us and direct us all through today.

Help us to work aright, so that every task may be so well done that we can take it and show it to you.
Help us to speak aright, and preserve us alike from too hasty speech and from cowardly silence.
Help us to think aright, and so guard our minds and hearts that no evil and no bitter thought may gain an entry in to them.

Help us to live as befits those who have begun this day with you, and who go out to live every moment of it in your presence. Grant that today our lives may shine like lights of love and goodness in the world that we may bring credit to the name we bear, and honour to the Master, whose we are and whom we seek to serve. This we ask for your love's sake. AMEN.

IN THE EVENING

O God, our Father, we thank you for today.

We thank you that you have given us strength and health of body and of mind to do our work and to earn a living.
We thank you for our loved ones, and for all our comrades and our friends, without whom life could never be the same.

O God, our Father, grant us your forgiveness for today.

Forgive us if today our work was badly done, no better than our second best.
Forgive us if today we failed a friend, or hurt and disappointed anyone who loves us.

And now, as we go to rest, grant us the peace of those who have cast all their burdens upon you, and who know that their times are always in your hand. This we ask for your love's sake.

AMEN.

DAILY READING

Psalm 116:1–8

I love the Lord, because he hath heard my voice *and* my supplications.

Because he hath inclined his ear unto me, therefore will I call upon him as long as I live.

The sorrows of death compassed me, and the pains of hell gat hold upon me: I found trouble and sorrow.

Then called I upon the name of the Lord; O Lord, I beseech thee, deliver my soul.

Gracious is the Lord, and righteous; yea, our God *is* merciful.

The Lord preserveth the simple: I was brought low, and he helped me.

Return unto thy rest, O my soul; for the Lord hath dealt bountifully with thee.

For thou hast delivered my soul from death, mine eyes from tears, and my feet from falling.

TWENTY-FIRST DAY

O God, our Father, grant that whatever happens to us today we may take it to you.

If we shall have decisions to make, help us to ask your guidance, and grant us humility and obedience to take it when you give it to us.
If we shall have problems to solve, help us to ask your light upon them, so that we may see a clear way through them.
If we shall have hard and difficult things to do, help us to ask for your strength, so that we may be enabled to do the things which we could not do ourselves.
If we shall have temptations to face, help us to seek your grace, remembering that Jesus, because he was tempted, is able to help others who are tempted.

Help us all through today to decide everything by your will, and to test everything by your presence, so that we may come to the day's ending without mistakes and without regrets: through Jesus Christ our Lord.   AMEN.

IN THE EVENING

O God, our Father, we give you thanks for every part of the day which is coming to an end.

We thank you for the morning light to call us from our resting beds.
We thank you for the midday hours filled with work and with many activities in the company of our fellow men and women.
We thank you for the evening time to sit at home amidst our family circle, or to go out upon our pleasures with our friends. And now we thank you for the night and for kindly sleep.

We thank you for every happy thing which has come to us this day, and for all things which bring us joy when we remember them.

We ask your forgiveness for everything in today which hurts us and shames us when we remember it.

Grant to us now to lay ourselves down, and to sleep in peace, because we are at peace with you, and at peace with our fellow men and women: through Jesus Christ our Lord. AMEN.

DAILY READING

Philippians 4:4–8

Rejoice in the Lord alway: and again I say, Rejoice. Let your moderation be known unto all men. The Lord is at hand. Be careful for nothing; but in every thing by prayer and supplication with thanksgiving let your requests be made known unto God. And the peace of God, which passeth all understanding, shall keep your hearts and minds through Christ Jesus. Finally, brethren, whatsoever things are true, whatsoever things are honest, whatsoever things are just, whatsoever things are pure, whatsoever things are lovely, whatsoever things are of good report; if there be any virtue, and if there be any praise, think on these things.

TWENTY-SECOND DAY

IN THE MORNING

O God, our Father, help us this day to treat all people aright.

Help us to be a good example to those who are younger than we are; to be respectful to those who are older than we are; and to be at all times courteous to our equals.

Help us to be obedient to those who are set in authority over us; and to be just and fair and kind to any over whom we have control.

Help us to be sympathetic to those in distress, to be helpful to those in trouble, and to be kind to those in need.

So make us all this day to go about doing good as our Master did. This we ask for your love's sake. AMEN.

IN THE EVENING

O God, our Father, if we have hurt anyone today, give us grace to say that we are sorry.

If we have been wrong in anything today, give us grace to admit our error.

If we have been resentful today, help us in the time to come to accept rebuke in the spirit of humility, even if we think that we do not deserve it.

If we have parted with anyone in anger today, or if there has been a misunderstanding between us and anyone else, give us grace to take the first step to put things right.

If we have been unjust or unfair, or, if we have said things in the heat of the moment which we would not have said if we had stopped to think, give us grace to apologize.

Help us this night, before we lay ourselves to sleep, to make up our minds that we will leave no breach between us and anyone else unhealed. This we ask for your love's sake. AMEN.

Joshua 1:6–9

Be strong and of a good courage: for unto this people shalt thou divide for an inheritance the land, which I sware unto their fathers to give them. Only be thou strong and very courageous, that thou mayest observe to do according to all the law, which Moses my servant commanded thee: turn not from it to the right hand or to the left, that thou mayest prosper whithersoever thou goest. This book of the law shall not depart out of thy mouth; but thou shalt meditate therein day and night, that thou mayest observe to do according to all that is written therein: for then thou shalt make thy way prosperous, and then thou shalt have good success. Have not I commanded thee? Be strong and of a good courage; be not afraid, neither be thou dismayed: for the Lord thy God is with thee whithersoever thou goest.

TWENTY-THIRD DAY

IN THE MORNING

O God, our Father, help us this day to work faithfully and to work well.

Grant that we may put off until tomorrow no task which should be done today.
Grant that we may not do with a grudge that which should be done with a smile.
Grant that we may never be content to render to anyone else that which is less than our best.

Help us all through this day to be as kind to others as we would wish them to be with us.
Help us always to be honest, never to be guilty of any mean action or any sharp practice, and never to seek an unfair advantage over others.

Help us all through this day to work in such a way that when the evening comes we shall hear you say: 'Well done!'

Hear this our prayer for your love's sake.   AMEN.

IN THE EVENING

O God, our Father, be with us as this day ends.

If we are feeling depressed, if we have honestly done our best and yet feel that we are a failure, help us to know that you understand.
If we are well aware that we have done something wrong today, save us from the foolishness of trying to hide it from you; and help us to tell you about it, knowing that, if we are truly sorry, you will forgive.
If things have hurt us today, if people have been unkind and

friends have been unfaithful, help us to remember that Jesus too knows what it is like, because he went through it.

If today has been a happy day, and life has been sweet, help us not to forget now to give you thanks.

Before we sleep, we give you thanks for all your goodness; we ask your pardon for all our sins and our mistakes; and we ask your blessing on ourselves and on those we love: through Jesus Christ our Lord. AMEN.

DAILY READING

Matthew 7:7–12

Ask, and it shall be given you; seek, and ye shall find; knock, and it shall be opened unto you: for every one that asketh receiveth; and he that seeketh findeth; and to him that knocketh it shall be opened. Or what man is there of you, whom if his son ask bread, will he give him a stone? Or if he ask a fish, will he give him a serpent? If ye then, being evil, know how to give good gifts unto your children, how much more shall your Father which is in heaven give good things to them that ask him? Therefore all things whatsoever ye would that men should do to you, do ye even so to them: for this is the law and the prophets.

TWENTY-FOURTH DAY

In the morning

O God, our Father, who has made all things and made them well, we thank you for sleep by night and for work by day.

We thank you for this world which you have made; for night and day; for light and dark; for sunset and for dawn.

We thank you that you have made us as we are. We thank you for hands to work and feet to walk; for eyes to see and ears to hear; for minds to think and plan, for memories to remember, and for hearts to love.

We thank you for those who today will teach us, for those to whom we will go for advice, and for those on whose wisdom and experience we will draw to help us to do our work, and to solve our problems.

We thank you for those whose friendship every day gives strength and whose love gives glory to our lives.

Above all else we thank you for Jesus Christ, our blessed Lord. Grant that all through today we may never forget his presence always with us. This we ask for your love's sake.   AMEN.

In the evening

O God, our Father, we remember before you those who dread and fear the night.

Bless those in pain and in distress of body; those who, although they are tired, cannot sleep; those whom worry has robbed of rest; those for whom the world seems very empty and very lonely at evening time; little children who are lonely and afraid of the dark.

Forgive us this night for all the wrong that we have this day done, even for the things for which we find it hard to forgive ourselves.

Grant us this night the mind at rest in the peace that passes understanding; the heart content in the love from which nothing can separate us; and the life which is hid with Christ in you.

This we ask for your love's sake. AMEN.

DAILY READING

Psalm 139:7–14

Whither shall I go from thy spirit? or whither shall I flee from thy presence?

If I ascend up into heaven, thou art there: if I make my bed in hell, behold, thou art there.

If I take the wings of the morning, and dwell in the uttermost parts of the sea;

Even there shall thy hand lead me, and thy right hand shall hold me.

If I say, Surely the darkness shall cover me; even the night shall be light about me.

Yea, the darkness hideth not from thee; but the night shineth as the day: the darkness and the light are both alike to thee.

For thou hast possessed my reins: thou hast covered me in my mother's womb.

I will praise thee; for I am fearfully and wonderfully made: marvellous are thy works; and that my soul knoweth right well.

TWENTY-FIFTH DAY

IN THE MORNING

O God, our Father, whose love is over every creature whom your hands have made, as we go out this morning to the world and our work we ask you to bless all classes and conditions of men and women everywhere.

Bless those who are servants, and help them to serve with diligence; and bless those who are masters, and help them to direct and to control with justice and with mercy.

Bless those who are rich, and help them to remember that they must hold all their possessions in stewardship for you; and bless those who are poor, and grant that they may find others kind.

Bless those who are strong and fit, and grant that they may never use their good health selfishly; and bless those who are weak and ailing, and keep them from all discouragement and discontent.

Bless those who are happy, and help them not to forget you in the sunny weather; and bless those who are sad, and ease the pain and comfort, the loneliness of their hearts.

Bless the animals who are the friends and the servants of men, and grant that none may treat them with cruelty, but that all may be kind to them.

Bless each one of us, and grant that we may go out to live as those who have been with Jesus. This we ask for your love's sake. AMEN.

IN THE EVENING

O God, our Father, who are plenteous in mercy, forgive us for all the wrong things which have spoiled today.

Forgive us for any moment when the voice of conscience spoke to us, and we heard it, but went our own way.

Forgive us for any moment when we forgot you; when we were so immersed in the affairs and the pleasures of this world that we had no thought to spare for you.

Forgive us for any moment when we grieved you; for any word or action or conduct which made men think less of the name we bear.

Forgive us if today we have neglected duty, failed in witness, wavered in faith, fallen away from love.

When we think of our own failure we thank you most of all for Jesus Christ, who gave his life a ransom for many, and who is the Lamb of God who takes away the sin of the world, and our sin. Grant that before we sleep we may find in him your pardon and your peace. This we ask for your love's sake.   AMEN.

DAILY READING

Matthew 7:16–20

Ye shall know them by their fruits. Do men gather grapes of thorns, or figs of thistles? Even so every good tree bringeth forth good fruit; but a corrupt tree bringeth forth evil fruit. A good tree cannot bring forth evil fruit, neither can a corrupt tree bring forth good fruit. Every tree that bringeth not forth good fruit is hewn down, and cast into the fire. Wherefore by their fruits ye shall know them.

TWENTY-SIXTH DAY

IN THE MORNING

O God, our Father, grant us your blessing as we go out to meet this day.

Grant us this day lips which speak the truth, but which ever speak the truth in love.

Grant us minds which seek the truth; and grant that we may face the truth even when it hurts and condemns us, and that we may never shut our eyes to that which we do not wish to see.

Grant us hands which work with diligence, and which yet have time to help another with his task.

Grant us resolution to stand for principle; but save us from stubbornness, and from magnifying trifles into principles.

Grant us grace to conquer our temptations and to live in purity; but save us from the self-righteousness which would look down on anyone who has fallen by the way.

All through this day grant us the strength and the gentleness of our blessed Lord. This we ask for your love's sake. AMEN.

IN THE EVENING

O God, our Father, there are things in today which make us ashamed when we remember them.

Forgive us if we have lost our temper with the people who get on our nerves.

Forgive us if we have been cross and irritable with those who are nearest and dearest to us.

Forgive us if at any time we were discourteous and impolite to those with whom we came in contact in our work.

Forgive us if we have thoughtlessly or deliberately hurt anyone's feelings today.

O God, our Father, there are things in today which make us glad when we remember them.

We thank you for any lovely thing that we have seen, for any wise thing that we have heard, and for any good thing that we have been enabled to do.
We thank you for the time we have spent with our friends and comrades, and with those we love.

O God, our Father, accept our sorrow for our sins and our gratitude for your gifts before we sleep this night: through Jesus Christ our Lord. AMEN.

DAILY READING

Isaiah 2:2–4

And it shall come to pass in the last days, that the mountain of the Lord's house shall be established in the top of the mountains, and shall be exalted above the hills; and all nations shall flow unto it. And many people shall go and say, Come ye, and let us go up to the mountain of the Lord, to the house of the God of Jacob; and he will teach us of his ways, and we will walk in his paths; for out of Zion shall go forth the law and the word of the Lord from Jerusalem. And he shall judge among the nations, and shall rebuke many people: and they shall beat their swords into plowshares, and their spears into pruninghooks: nation shall not lift up sword against nation, neither shall they learn war any more.

TWENTY-SEVENTH DAY

IN THE MORNING

O God, our Father, help us all through this day to obey your law, and to do to others all that we would wish them to do to us.

Grant to us to help others, as we would wish them to help us, when we are in difficulty or in distress.

Help us to forgive others as we would wish them to forgive us when we make mistakes.
Help us to make the same allowances for others as we would wish them to make for us.
Help us to have the same sympathy for others as we would wish them to have for us when we are sad.
Help us to have the same respect and tolerance for the views and for the beliefs of others as we would wish them to have for ours.
Help us to try to understand others as we would wish to be understood

Help us so to enter into others that we may see things with their eyes, and think things with their minds, and feel things with their hearts; and so grant that we may be as kind to others as we would wish them to be to us: through Jesus Christ our Lord.
AMEN.

IN THE EVENING

O God, our Father, bless those for whom life is unhappy.

Bless those who are underpaid and overworked, those who never have enough, and who are always tired.
Bless those who are always taken for granted, and who are never thanked, and praised, and appreciated, as they ought to be.
Bless those who have been hurt by life, those who have been wounded by the malice of their enemies, or by the faithlessness of their friends.

Bless those who have been disappointed in something on which they had set their hearts.

Bless those for whom life is lonely and empty, because someone they loved has been taken away.

Bless those whom illness or weakness has handicapped or laid aside.

Bless those who are worried about those they love.

You know the needs of each one of us, and you know the secrets of our inmost hearts. Help us this night to cast all our burdens upon you, certain that you care for us, and sure that you will help. This we ask for your love's sake. AMEN.

DAILY READING

John 3:14–17

And as Moses lifted up the serpent in the wilderness, even so must the Son of man be lifted up: that whosoever believeth in him should not perish, but have eternal life. For God so loved the world, that he gave his only begotten Son, that whosoever believeth in him should not perish, but have everlasting life. For God sent not his Son into the world to condemn the world; but that the world through him might be saved.

TWENTY-EIGHTH DAY

IN THE MORNING

O God, our Father, grant to us all through this day to do not what we like but what we ought. Grant to us all through this day to follow your will and not our own desires.

Help us to do with diligence the tasks we do not wish to do.
Help us to meet with graciousness the people we do not like to meet.
Help us in all things to set duty above pleasure.

Grant that conscience may be our only master, and that our only motive may be to do things well enough to take them and to show them to you.
Grant to us never to seek to do as little as possible and to get as much as possible; never to seek to evade our work; never to leave to others that which we ourselves should do; never to avoid the decisions we ought to make, or to shirk the responsibilities we ought to shoulder.

So grant that at the evening time we may know the deep contentment of work completed and of duty done: through Jesus Christ our Lord. AMEN.

IN THE EVENING

O God, our Father, forgive us for everything in this day which has grieved you to see.

Forgive us if we have made the work of others harder instead of easier.
Forgive us if we have discouraged others instead of encouraging them.
Forgive us if our presence has depressed others instead of making them happier.

Forgive us if we have grumbled and complained, and so made things unhappy for ourselves and for everyone else.

Forgive us if we have been cross, irritable, bad-tempered, fault-finding, and difficult to live with.

Forgive us if we have made it easier for someone else to do wrong, and harder for him to do right.

Forgive us if we have been ungracious and ungrateful.

Forgive us if we have worried our friends, or hurt our loved ones.

Forgive us for all the things of which we are now ashamed, and give us grace tomorrow to walk more closely to you; through Jesus Christ our Lord.   AMEN.

DAILY READING

Psalm 24:1–5

The earth is the Lord's, and the fulness thereof; the world, and they that dwell therein.

For he hath founded it upon the seas, and established it upon the floods.

Who shall ascend into the hill of the Lord? or who shall stand in his holy place?

He that hath clean hands, and a pure heart; who hath not lifted up his soul unto vanity, nor sworn deceitfully.

He shall receive the blessing from the Lord, and righteousness from the God of his salvation.

TWENTY-NINTH DAY

IN THE MORNING

O God, our Father, help us to learn the lessons that life is seeking
  to teach us.

Save us from making the same mistakes over and over again.
Save us from falling to the same temptations time and time again.
Save us from doing things that we should not do, until the doing
  of them has become a habit which we cannot break.
Save us from failing to realize our own weaknesses, and from
  refusing to see our own faults.
Save us from persisting in courses of action which we ought to
  have learned long ago can lead to nothing but trouble.
Save us from doing things which we know annoy other people.

Help us daily to grow stronger, purer, kinder.
Help us daily to shed old faults, and to gain new virtues, until,
  by your grace, life becomes altogether new.

Hear this our morning prayer for your love's sake.   AMEN.

IN THE EVENING

O God, our Father, we thank you for this day.

We thank you for those who have given us guidance, counsel,
  advice and good example.
We thank you for those in whose company the sun shone even
  in the rain, and who brought a smile to our faces even when
  things were grim.
We thank you for those in whose company the frightening things
  were not so alarming, and the hard things not so difficult.
We thank you for those whose presence saved us from falling to
  temptation, and enabled us to do the right.
We thank you for those whom it is joy even to be with, and in

whose company the hours pass all too quickly.

We thank you for happy times to be to us for ever happy memories.

We thank you for times of failure to keep us humble, and to make us remember how much we need you.

Most of all we thank you for Jesus Christ, who in the daytime is our friend and our companion and who in the night is our pillow and our peace.

Hear this our evening thanksgiving for your love's sake. AMEN.

DAILY READING

Romans 12:10–16

Be kindly affectioned one to another with brotherly love; in honour preferring one another; Not slothful in business; fervent in spirit; serving the Lord; Rejoicing in hope; patient in tribulation; continuing instant in prayer; Distributing to the necessity of saints; given to hospitality. Bless them which persecute you: bless, and curse not. Rejoice with them that do rejoice, and weep with them that weep. Be of the same mind one toward another. Mind not high things, but condescend to men of low estate. Be not wise in your own conceits.

THIRTIETH DAY

IN THE MORNING

O God, our Father, equip us with these gifts of yours which will enable us to live aright today and every day.

Grant us the faith which can accept the things which it cannot understand, and which will never turn to doubt.
Grant us the hope which still hopes on, even in the dark, and which will never turn to despair.
Grant us the loyalty which will be true to you, even though all men deny you, and which will never stoop to compromise.
Grant us the purity which can resist all the seductions of temptation, and which can never be turned from the straight way.

Arm our wills with your strength, and fill our hearts with your love, so that we may be strong to obey you and loving to serve our fellow men and women, and so be like our Master. This we ask for your love's sake. AMEN.

IN THE EVENING

O God, our Father, we remember all the failures of today.

Forgive us for any promises we broke today, or any resolutions we failed to keep.
Forgive us for any friends we failed today, or any people we hurt.
Forgive us for any carelessness in our work today, or any neglect of duty.
Forgive us for any mean, ungenerous, or dishonourable deed today, for any false, impure, or angry word.

O God, our Father, we remember all who have helped us today.

We thank you for those who helped us with our work.

We thank you for those who helped us to resist our temptations.
We thank you for anyone who gave us a word of thanks, of encouragment, of praise, or of appreciation.
We thank you for those who sent us happier on our way, because we met them.

More than anything else we thank you for Jesus, our Saviour and our Friend.

Grant that we may show our penitence for our failures, and our gratitude for your gifts by waking to do better tomorrow, and to walk more closely with you. This we ask for your love's sake. AMEN.

DAILY READING

Isaiah 1:16–18

Wash you, make you clean; put away the evil of your doings from before mine eyes; cease to do evil; Learn to do well; seek judgement, relieve the oppressed, judge the fatherless, plead for the widow. Come now, and let us reason together, saith the Lord: though your sins be as scarlet, they shall be as white as snow; though they be red like crimson, they shall be as wool.

THIRTY-FIRST DAY

In the morning

Help me, O God, to meet in the right way and in the right spirit everything which comes to me today.

Help me to approach my work cheerfully, and my tasks diligently.

Help me to meet people courteously, and, if need be, to suffer fools gladly.

Help me to meet disappointments, frustrations, hindrances, opposition, calmly and without irritation.

Help me to meet delays with patience, and unreasonable demands with self-control.

Help me to accept praise modestly, and criticism without losing my temper.

Keep me serene all through today.

All this I ask for Jesus' sake.   AMEN.

In the evening

O God, bless those whose faces come into my mind as I come into your presence.

Bless those whom I love; if it be possible, let nothing happen to them.

Bless my friends, and the people beside whom I work; let nothing come between me and them.

Bless those whom I know to be ill; give them restful and healing sleep tonight.

Bless those whom I know to be sad; and comfort them.

Bless those who are being very foolish; keep them from doing anything that would wreck life for themselves and for others.

Bless the poor, the homeless, the friendless, those in prison, in misfortune and in disgrace.

Bless my absent friends; bless those who are away from home.

You are the Father of all. In your fatherly love bless all who need your blessing.

This I ask for your love's sake.   AMEN.

DAILY READING

John 1:1–5, 11–14

In the beginning was the Word, and the Word was with God, and the Word was God. The same was in the beginning with God. All things were made by him; and without him was not any thing made that was made. In him was life; and the life was the light of men. And the light shineth in darkness; and the darkness comprehended it not. He came unto his own, and his own received him not. But as many as received him, to them gave he power to become the sons of God, even to them that believe on his name: which were born, not of blood, nor of the will of the flesh, nor of the will of man, but of God. And the Word was made flesh, and dwelt among us, (and we beheld his glory, the glory as of the only begotten of the Father,) full of grace and truth.

THIRTY-SECOND DAY

In the Morning

O God, help me today to think of the feelings of others as much
as I think of my own.
If I know that there are things which annoy the people with whom
I live and work, help me not to do them.
If I know that there are things which would please them, help me
to go out of my way to do them.
Help me to think before I speak, so that I may not thoughtlessly
or tactlessly hurt or embarrass anyone else.
If I have to differ with anyone, help me to do so with courtesy.
If I have to argue with anyone, help me to do so without losing
my temper.
If I have to find fault with anyone, help me to do so with kindness.
If anyone has to find fault with me, help me to accept it with a
good grace.
Help me all through today to treat others as I would wish them
to treat me: through Jesus Christ my Lord.   AMEN.

In the Evening

O God, bless the people who are thinking of me and praying for
me tonight.
my parents, my family, my friends, my loved ones.
Bless those who have no one to remember them, and no one to
pray for them,
the aged, the lonely, the friendless, those who have no one to
love and no one to love them.
Bless those who specially need my remembrance and my prayers,
those in illness and in pain, those whose life is in the balance,
those who are dying, those who are in bewilderment, those
who are in regret and remorse, those who have been driven
to despair.

Bless me before I sleep, and grant me now
A grateful heart for all your gifts;
A contrite heart for all my sins;
A heart at peace, because it rests in you.
Hear this my prayer for your love's sake. AMEN.

DAILY READING

Psalm 46

God *is* our refuge and strength, a very present help in trouble.
Therefore will not we fear, though the earth be removed, and
though the mountains be carried into the midst of the sea;
Though the waters thereof roar and be troubled, though the
mountains shake with the swelling thereof. Selah.
There is a river, the streams whereof shall make glad the city of
God, the holy place of the tabernacles of the most High. God
is in the midst of her; she shall not be moved: God shall help
her, and that right early.
The heathen raged, the kingdoms were moved: he uttered his
voice, the earth melted.
The Lord of hosts is with us; the God of Jacob is our refuge. Selah.
Come, behold the works of the Lord, what desolations he hath
made in the earth.
He maketh wars to cease unto the end of the earth; he breaketh
the bow, and cutteth the spear in sunder; he burneth the chariot
in the fire.
Be still, and know that I am God: I will be exalted among the
heathen, I will be exalted in the earth.
The Lord of hosts is with us; the God of Jacob is our refuge. Selah.

THIRTY-THIRD DAY

All through today, O God, help me to be,
  Quick to praise, and slow to criticize;
  Quick to forgive, and slow to condemn;
  Quick to share, and slow to refuse to give.

Grant me all through today,
  Complete control over my temper,
    that I may be slow to anger;
  Complete control over my tongue,
    that I may speak no hasty word.

So grant that all through today I may help everyone and hurt no
  one, so that I may find true joy in living: through Jesus Christ
  my Lord. AMEN.

O God, my Father, as I lay me down to sleep,
  Relax the tension of my body;
  Calm the restlessness of my mind;
  Still the thoughts which worry and perplex.
Help me to rest myself and all my problems in the clasp of your
  everlasting arms.
Let your Spirit speak to my mind and my heart while I am asleep,
  so that, when I waken in the morning, I may find that I have
  received in the night-time

  Light for my way;
  Strength for my tasks;
  Peace for my worries;
  Forgiveness for my sins.

Grant me sleep tonight, and tomorrow power to live.
This I ask through Jesus Christ my Lord. AMEN.

Matthew 10:24–31

The disciple is not above his master, nor the servant above his lord. It is enough for the disciple that he be as his master, and the servant as his lord. If they have called the master of the house Beelzebub, how much more shall they call them of his household? Fear them not therefore: for there is nothing covered, that shall not be revealed; and hid, that shall not be known. What I tell you in darkness, that speak ye in light: and what ye hear in the ear, that preach ye upon the housetops. And fear not them which kill the body, but are not able to kill the soul: but rather fear him which is able to destroy both soul and body in hell. Are not two sparrows sold for a farthing? and one of them shall not fall on the ground without your Father. But the very hairs of your head are all numbered. Fear ye not therefore, ye are of more value than many sparrows.

THIRTY-FOURTH DAY

Equip me today, O God, with

The humility, which will keep me from pride and from conceit;
The graciousness and the gentleness, which will make me both
easy to live with and a joy to meet;
The diligence, and perseverance, and the reliability, which will
make me a good workman;
The kindness which will give me a quick eye to see what I can
do for others, and a ready hand to do it;
The constant awareness of your presence, which will make me
do everything as unto you.

So grant that today men may see in me a glimpse of the life of
my Blessed Lord.
This I ask for your love's sake. AMEN.

Thank you, O God, for all the help you have given me today.

Thank you for
Keeping me safe all through today;
Helping me to do my work all through today;
Giving me strength to conquer my temptations all through today.

Thank you for
My home and all that it has been to me;
My loved ones and all the circle of those most dear;
My friends and comrades with whom I have worked and talked.

Thank you for
Any kindness I have received;
Any help that was given to me;

Any sympathy that was shown to me.

Help me to lay myself down to sleep tonight with a glad and
grateful heart.

This I ask through Jesus Christ my Lord.   AMEN.

Psalm 63:1–7

O God, thou art my God; early will I seek thee: my soul thirsteth
for thee, my flesh longeth for thee in a dry and thirsty land,
where no water is;

To see thy power and thy glory, so as I have seen thee in the
sanctuary.

Because thy lovingkindness is better than life, my lips shall praise
thee.

Thus will I bless thee while I live: I will lift up my hands in thy
name.

My soul shall be satisfied as with marrow and fatness; and my
mouth shall praise thee with joyful lips:

When I remember thee upon my bed, and meditate on thee in
the night watches.

Because thou hast been my help, therefore in the shadow of thy
wings will I rejoice.

THIRTY-FIFTH DAY

O God, help me all through today
  To do nothing to worry those who love me;
  To do nothing to let down those who trust me;
  To do nothing to fail those who employ me;
  To do nothing to hurt those who are close to me.

Help me all through this day
  To do nothing which would be a cause of temptation to
    someone else or which would make it easier for someone
    else to go wrong;
  Not to discourage anyone who is doing his best;
  Not to dampen anyone's enthusiasms, or to increase anyone's
    doubts.

Help me all through this day
  To be a comfort to the sad;
  To be a friend to the lonely;
  To be an encouragement to the dispirited;
  To be a help to those who are up against it.

So grant that others may see in me something of the reflection
  of the Master whose I am and whom I seek to serve.

This I ask for your love's sake. AMEN.

Forgive me, O God, if today
  By being irritable and unreasonable, I made trouble in the family
    circle;
  By being careless and slack and inefficient at my work, I made
    the tasks of others more difficult;
  By being self-willed and stubborn and too set on my own way,

I was a problem to my friends and my companions.

Forgive me if today
I was too impatient with someone who was doing his best;
I have been too quick to take offence, and to see slights where
no slight was intended;
I did things badly, and caused others trouble, because I was not
attending to my instructions and to my work as I ought to have
been.

Help me tomorrow to be more strict with myself; more
understanding to others; more faithful to my work than ever
before: through Jesus Christ my Lord. AMEN.

Matthew 13:31–4

Another parable put he forth unto them, saying, The kingdom of
heaven is like to a grain of mustard seed, which a man took, and
sowed in his field; Which indeed is the least of all seeds: but when
it is grown, it is the greatest among herbs, and becometh a tree,
so that the birds of the air come and lodge in the branches thereof.
Another parable spake he unto them: The kingdom of heaven is
like unto leaven, which a woman took, and hid in three measures
of meal, till the whole was leavened. All these things spake Jesus
unto the multitude in parables; and without a parable spake he
not unto them.

THIRTY-SIXTH DAY

IN THE MORNING

O God, I know that I am going to be very busy today. Help me not to be so busy that I miss the most important things.

Help me not to be too busy to look up and to see a glimpse of beauty in your world.

Help me not to be too busy listening to other voices to hear your voice when you speak to me.

Help me not to be too busy to listen to anyone who is in trouble, and to help anyone who is in difficulty.

Help me not to be too busy to stand still for a moment to think and to remember.

Help me not to be too busy to remember the claims of my home, my children, and my family.

Help me all through today to remember that I must work my hardest, and also to remember that sometimes I must be still.

This I ask for Jesus' sake.   AMEN.

IN THE EVENING

O God, sometimes I begin to worry, especially when I sit at the end of the day and think.

I begin to worry about my work.
   Help me to know that with your help I can cope.

I begin to worry about money, and about making ends meet. Help me to remember that, though money is important, there are things that money cannot buy – and these are the most precious things of all.

I begin to worry about my health.
Help me to remember that worrying makes me worse, and that trusting always makes me better.

I begin to worry about the things which tempt me.
Help me to remember that you are with me to help me to conquer them.

I begin to worry about those I love.
Help me to do everything I can for them, and then to leave them in your care.

Give me tonight your peace in my troubled heart: through Jesus Christ my Lord. AMEN.

DAILY READING

Psalm 51:7–12

Purge me with hyssop, and I shall be clean: wash me, and I shall be whiter than snow.

Make me to hear joy and gladness; that the bones which thou hast broken may rejoice.

Hide thy face from my sins, and blot out all mine iniquities.

Create in me a clean heart, O God: and renew a right spirit within me.

Cast me not away from thy presence; and take not thy holy spirit from me.

Restore unto me the joy of thy salvation; and uphold me with thy free spirit.

THIRTY-SEVENTH DAY

In the morning

Lord Jesus, help me to walk with you all through today.

Give me today
  Something of the wisdom that was in your words;
  Something of the love that was in your heart;
  Something of the help that was on your hands.

Give me today
  Something of your patience with people;
  Something of your ability to bear slights and insults and
    injuries without bitterness and without resentment;
  Something of your ability always to forgive.

Help me to live in such a way today that others may know that
  I began the day with you, and that I am walking with you, so
  that, however dimly, others may see you in me.

This I ask for your love's sake.   AMEN.

In the evening

O God, I think tonight of those in special trouble and distress of
  body, mind, or heart.

Bless the homes in which someone has died, and in which those
  who are left are bewildered and sad.

Bless the homes where tonight there are those who must sit by
  the bed of a loved one and wait for the end to come.

Bless those who are ill, and whose pain seems worst of all in the
  slow night hours.

Bless homes into which bad news has come, homes in which
  some member of the family has brought shame upon himself

and sorrow to those who love him.

Bless those who are sitting alone with some bitter disappointment, with some dream that has ended, and which will now never come true.

Bless those for whom life has fallen in.

Bless those who are wrestling with some temptation, and those who have lost the battle.

Bless those who are separated from those they love, and who are lonely and anxious.

Where there is trouble of any kind, be there to comfort and support.

This I ask for your love's sake.   AMEN.

DAILY READING

Matthew 11:25–30

At that time Jesus answered and said, I thank thee, O Father, Lord of heaven and earth, because thou hast hid these things from the wise and prudent, and hast revealed them unto babes. Even so, Father: for so it seemed good in thy sight. All things are delivered unto me of my Father: and no man knoweth the Son, but the Father; neither knoweth any man the Father, save the Son, and he to whomsoever the Son will reveal him. Come unto me, all ye that labour and are heavy laden, and I will give you rest. Take my yoke upon you, and learn of me; for I am meek and lowly in heart; and ye shall find rest unto your souls. For my yoke is easy, and my burden is light.

THIRTY-EIGHTH DAY

O God, Lord of all good life, help me to use today well.

Help me to use today
  To know you a little better;
  To do my work a little more diligently;
  To serve my fellow men and women a little more lovingly;
  To make myself by your help a little more like Jesus.

Help me to make today a day of progress in my life, and to become a little more like what you want me to be.

This I ask for Jesus' sake. AMEN.

Forgive me, O Father, for anything I refused to do today which I might have done.

Forgive me for any help I might have given today, and did not give.

Forgive me for being so wrapped up in my own troubles and my own problems that I had no time for those of anyone else.

Forgive me for being so immersed in my own work that I had no time to give anyone else a helping hand.

Forgive me for selfishly hoarding my own leisure and comfort, and for refusing to give them up to help others, or to help your Church and your people and your work.

Help me to learn the lesson – I know that it is true – that selfishness and happiness can never go together; and help me to find happiness in trying to forget myself, and in trying to bring help and happiness to others: through Jesus Christ my Lord. AMEN.

Psalm 34:1–8

I will bless the Lord at all times: his praise shall continually be in my mouth.

My soul shall make her boast in the Lord; the humble shall hear thereof, and be glad.

O magnify the Lord with me, and let us exalt his name together.

I sought the Lord, and he heard me, and delivered me from all my fears.

They looked unto him, and were lightened: and their faces were not ashamed.

This poor man cried, and the Lord heard him, and saved him out of all his troubles.

The angel of the Lord encampeth round about them that fear him, and delivereth them.

O taste and see that the Lord is good: blessed is the man that trusteth in him.

THIRTY-NINTH DAY

Give me this day, O God,
   The energy I need to face my work;
   The diligence I need to do it well;
   The self-discipline, which will make me work just as hard, even
      if there be none to see, and none to praise, and none to blame;
   The self-respect which will not stoop to produce anything
      which is less than my best;
   The courtesy and the considerateness which will make me easy
      to live with and easy to work with.

Help me so to live today that I may make this world a happier
   place wherever I may be: through Jesus Christ my Lord.

AMEN.

Give me this night, O Father, the peace of mind which is truly rest.

Take from me
   All envy of anyone else;
   All resentment for anything which has been withheld from me;
   All bitterness against anyone who has hurt me or wronged me;
   All anger against the apparent injustice of life;
   All foolish worry about the future, and all futile regret about the
      past.

Help me to be
   At peace with myself;
   At peace with my fellow men and women;
   At peace with you.

So indeed may I lay myself down to rest in peace: through Jesus
   Christ my Lord.   AMEN.

Matthew 6:27–34

Which of you by taking thought can add one cubit unto his stature? And why take ye thought for raiment? Consider the lilies of the field, how they grow; they toil not, neither do they spin: And yet I say unto you, That even Solomon in all his glory was not arrayed like one of these. Wherefore, if God so clothe the grass of the field, which today is, and tomorrow is cast into the oven, shall he not much more clothe you, O ye of little faith? Therefore take no thought, saying, What shall we eat? or, What shall we drink? or, Wherewithal shall we be clothed? (For after all these things do the Gentiles seek:) for your heavenly Father knoweth that ye have need of all these things. But seek ye first the kingdom of God, and his righteousness; and all these things shall be added unto you. Take therefore no thought for the morrow: for the morrow shall take thought for the things of itself. Sufficient unto the day is the evil thereof.

FORTIETH DAY

O God, give me strength and wisdom to live this day as I ought.

Give me
   Strength to conquer every temptation which will come to me;
   Strength to do every task which is assigned to me;
   Strength to shoulder every responsibility which is laid upon me.

Give me
   Wisdom to know when to speak, and when to keep silent;
   Wisdom to know when to act, and when to refrain from action;
   Wisdom to know when to speak my mind, and when to hold
   my peace.

So bring me to the end of this day in goodness, in happiness and
in content: through Jesus Christ my Lord. AMEN.

IN THE EVENING

O God, I know that there is nothing so precious as friendship and
that there is nothing so enriching as love.
Thank you for all the friends whom I have met today.
Thank you for all the people with whom I travelled, with whom
I walked, with whom I worked, with whom I talked, with
whom I ate.
Thank you for the people with whom I listened to music, or
watched plays or pictures, or watched games or played games.
Thank you for those who are even closer to me than my friends,
those whom I love, and those who love me; those whose hands
serve my needs and care for my comfort; those whose love
surrounds me all my days.
Help me always to be loyal to my friends and true to those who
love me: through Jesus Christ my Lord. AMEN.

Psalm 90:12–17

So teach *us* to number our days, that we may apply *our* hearts unto wisdom.

Return, O Lord, how long? and let it repent thee concerning thy servants.

O satisfy us early with thy mercy; that we may rejoice and be glad all our days.

Make us glad according to the days wherein thou has afflicted us, and the years wherein we have seen evil.

Let thy work appear unto thy servants, and thy glory unto their children.

And let the beauty of the Lord our God be upon us; and establish thou the work of our hands upon us; yea, the work of our hands establish thou it.

FORTY-FIRST DAY

O God, I want to try to begin today by thinking not of myself but
of others.

Bless those for whom today is going to be a difficult day:
Those who must make decisions;
Those who must wrestle with temptations;
Those who have some special problem to solve.

Bless those for whom today is going to be a sad day:
Those who are meeting the day with tears in their eyes and with
sorrow and loneliness in their hearts;
Those who today must lay some dear one to rest in death;
Those who awake to the morning with no work to do.

Bless those for whom today is going to be a happy day:
Those who are happy and who are eagerly looking forward to
today;
Those who are to be married today;
Those who will walk in the sunshine of life today.

Give me all through today sympathy and love for all, that I
may always try to weep with those who weep and to rejoice with
those who rejoice: through Jesus Christ my Lord. AMEN.

IN THE EVENING

O God, I thank you for today.
I thank you that you gave me

Health and strength and ability to do my work;
Friends with whom to walk and talk;
Those who love me, who care for me, and who pray for me.

I thank you
  For the times when you made me able to overcome my
  temptations;
  For the times when you made me able to choose the right and
  to refuse the wrong;
  For the times when you spoke to me, and gripped me, and kept
  me from doing something which would have brought me
  shame or regret.

I thank you for Jesus,
  For his example;
  For his presence with me;
  For the friendship I have with you because of him.

Help me to show my gratitude by loving you more and by serving
  and obeying you better: through Jesus Christ my Lord.   AMEN.

DAILY READING

John 14:1–6

Let not your heart be troubled: ye believe in God, believe also in
me. In my Father's house are many mansions: if it were not so,
I would have told you. I go to prepare a place for you. And if I
go and prepare a place for you, I will come again, and receive you
unto myself; that where I am, there ye may be also. And whither
I go ye know, and the way ye know. Thomas saith unto him, Lord,
we know not whither thou goest; and how can we know the way?
Jesus saith unto him, I am the way, the truth, and the life: no man
cometh unto the Father, but by me.

FORTY-SECOND DAY

———

O God, thank you for giving me another day, and another gift of
time.

Help me all through today not to put off until tomorrow that which
I ought to do today.

Help me not to put things off
Because I can't be bothered doing them;
Because I don't want to do them;
Because I don't like doing them;
Because I am afraid to do them.

Help me to do each task, to face each duty, to shoulder each
responsibility as it comes to me, so that, if life should end
tonight for me, there will be no loose ends, no things half-
finished, no tasks undone: through Jesus Christ my
Lord. AMEN.

When I sit down and think at night, O Father, before I go to sleep,
I always feel that there never has been a day when I have done
all that I meant to do, and when I have been all that I meant
to be. Somehow the day is never long enough, and my strength
of will is never strong enough. Even in spite of my many failures
keep me from discouragement; keep me from lowering my
ideals; keep me from abandoning hope and from giving up.

Help me to try still harder; to trust still more and more in you,
and less and less in myself.

This I ask for your love's sake. AMEN.

———

Psalm 95:1–6

O come, let us sing unto the Lord: let us make a joyful noise to the rock of our salvation.

Let us come before his presence with thanksgiving, and make a joyful noise unto him with psalms.

For the Lord is a great God, and a great King above all gods.

In his hand are the deep places of the earth: the strength of the hills is his also.

The sea is his, and he made it: and his hands formed the dry land.

O come, let us worship and bow down: let us kneel before the Lord our maker.

FORTY-THIRD DAY

O God, my Father, I am very fortunate in my home, my parents,
my family, my friends, my work, my church, my country. Today,
before I go out to work, I want to remember before you those
for whom life is not nearly so happy as it is for me:

Refugees who have no home, no place to call their own;
People in lands in which coloured people have no rights;
Those who love freedom in lands where freedom is lost;
Christians in lands where Christians are persecuted;
Those who are unhappy in their work, badly paid, compelled
to work in bad conditions;
Those who are treated at home without sympathy, and even
with cruelty;
Those who live or work in a situation in which it is very difficult
to be a Christian at all;
The friendless, the lonely, and the sad;
Those in hospitals and in places for those whose minds have
lost the light of reason;
Those in prison and in disgrace.

O God, grant that my own happiness may never make me blind
to the need and forgetful of the unhappiness of others: This
I ask for your love's sake. AMEN.

IN THE EVENING

Forgive me, O God
If today I have been too impatient, especially with people;
If today I have made anyone feel a nuisance;
If today in my heart of hearts I have thought people fools – and
have shown them that I did;

If today there were times when I was too aggressively sure that
  I was right;
If today I have ridden rough-shod over the feelings of someone
  else;
If today I have been
  Unapproachable to talk to;
  Difficult to work with;
  Unsympathetic to appeal to;
  Critical in my outlook;
  Harsh in my judgment.

I cannot undo what I have done, but help me tomorrow to be more
  loving and more kind – more like Jesus.

This I ask for your love's sake. AMEN.

DAILY READING

John 15:1–5

I am the true vine, and my Father is the husbandman. Every
branch in me that beareth not fruit he taketh away; and every
branch that beareth fruit, he purgeth it, that it may bring forth
more fruit. Now ye are clean through the word which I have
spoken unto you. Abide in me and I in you. As the branch cannot
bear fruit of itself, except it abide in the vine; no more can ye,
except ye abide in me. I am the vine, ye are the branches: he that
abideth in me, and I in him, the same bringeth forth much fruit:
for without me ye can do nothing.

FORTY-FOURTH DAY

O God, my Father, as I go out to life and work today,

I thank you for the world's beauty:
  For the light of the sun;
  For the wind on my face;
  For the colour of the flowers;
  And for all glimpses of lovely things.

I thank you for life's gracious things:
  For friendship's help;
  For kinship's strength;
  For love's wonder.

I remember this world's evil and its sin.
  Help me to overcome every temptation, and make my life like
  a light which guides to goodness. And, if anyone has fallen, help
  me to sympathize and to help rather than to judge and
  condemn.

I remember this world's sorrow.
  Help me today to bring comfort to some broken heart, and cheer
  to some lonely life.

So grant that, when evening comes, I may feel that I have not
  wasted this day.

Hear this my prayer through Jesus Christ my Lord.   AMEN.

IN THE EVENING

O God, my Father, tonight I bring to you myself, my life and all
  that is in it.

I bring to you
  My sins for your forgiveness;
  My hopes, my aims, my ambitions for your blessing;
  My temptations for your strength;
  My tasks, my duties, my responsibilities for your help;
  My friends, my dear ones, my loved ones for your care and your
  protection;
  And I bring everything with a thankful and a grateful heart for
  all that you have done for me.

So grant to me to sleep tonight with the everlasting arms
  underneath and about me: through Jesus Christ my
  Lord. AMEN.

DAILY READING

Psalm 100

Make a joyful noise unto the Lord, all ye lands.

Serve the Lord with gladness: come before his presence with
  singing.

Know ye that the Lord he is God: it is he that hath made us, and
  not we ourselves; we are his people, and the sheep of his
  pasture.

Enter into his gates with thanksgiving, and into his courts with
  praise: be thankful unto him, and bless his name.

For the Lord is good: his mercy is everlasting; and his truth
  endureth to all generations.

FORTY-FIFTH DAY

IN THE MORNING

O God, my Father, keep me from all failure all through today.

Keep me from
  Failure in gratitude to those to whom I owe so much;
  Failure in diligence to those to whom I owe my duty and my
  work;
  Failure in self-control, when temptation comes and when
  passions are strong.

Keep me from
  Failure to give my help to those who need my help;
  Failure to give an example and a lead to those who need support
  in goodness;
  Failure in kindness to those who are in trouble of any kind.

Help me this day perfectly to fulfil my responsibilities to myself,
  to my loved ones, to my employers, to my fellow men and
  women and to you.

This I ask for Jesus' sake.   AMEN.

IN THE EVENING

O God, you are the Father of all, and I ask your blessing on all
  those who are in trouble tonight.

I ask you to bless and help
  Little children who are afraid of the dark;
  Sufferers who cannot sleep for their pain;
  Those who in sorrow are lonelier than ever they thought it
  possible to be.

I ask you to bless and help
  Those in prison and in disgrace;

Those who have suddenly realized the mess they have made
of life for themselves and for others;

Those who have been hurt, wounded, failed, by those whom
they trusted, those in whom they believed, those whom they
loved;

Those who have newly come to see the sorrow and the
heartbreak of which their thoughtlessness has been the cause.

O God, my Father, bless me now before I sleep.

Thank you for today and for all the happy things that were in it.

Forgive me for anything in it which was wrong, and which grieved
others or hurt you.

Give me now a good night's rest and quiet sleep.

This I ask for Jesus' sake.   AMEN.

DAILY READING

Luke 9:57–62

And it came to pass, that, as they went in the way, a certain man
said unto him, Lord, I will follow thee whithersoever thou goest.
And Jesus said unto him, Foxes have holes, and birds of the air
have nests; but the Son of man hath not where to lay his head.
And he said unto another, Follow me. But he said, Lord, suffer
me first to go and bury my father. Jesus said unto him, Let the
dead bury their dead: but go thou and preach the Kingdom of
God. And another also said, Lord, I will follow thee; but let me
first go bid them farewell, which are at home at my house. And
Jesus said unto him, No man, having put his hand to the plough,
and looking back, is fit for the Kingdom of God.

FORTY-SIXTH DAY

Eternal and everblessed God, whom to know is life eternal,

Help me daily to know you better, that daily I may more fully enter into real life, and may more fully know the meaning of life.

Eternal and everblessed God, whom to serve is perfect freedom,

Grant that I may daily serve you more faithfully, so that in doing your will I may find my peace.

Eternal and everblessed God, whom to love is fullness of joy, Help me day by day to love you more, so that I may come a little nearer to loving you as you first loved me.

Hear this my prayer, through Jesus Christ my Lord. AMEN.

In the evening

O God, forgive me for allowing any wrong thoughts to enter into my mind today.

Forgive me for allowing my eyes to linger on things at which I should not even have looked.

Forgive me for speaking words which I should never have allowed to soil my lips.

Forgive me for needlessly giving temptation a chance to attack me.

Forgive me for all the things for which I am sorry now, and grant to me, before I sleep, the sense of being forgiven and the kiss of pardon and of peace.

This I ask for your love's sake. AMEN.

Psalm 124

If it had not been the Lord who was on our side, now may Israel
say;

If it had not been the Lord who was on our side, when men rose
up against us:

Then they had swallowed us up quick, when their wrath was
kindled against us:

Then the waters had overwhelmed us, the stream had gone over
our soul:

Then the proud waters had gone over our soul.

Blessed be the Lord, who hath not given us as a prey to their teeth.

Our soul is escaped as a bird out of the snare of the fowlers; the
snare is broken, and we are escaped.

Our help is in the name of the Lord, who made heaven and earth.

FORTY-SEVENTH DAY

O God, Father and Protector of all, bless all those for whom this
will be a worrying and a difficult day:

People in hospital, waiting to undergo an operation today;
People who must take some very important decision today;
Scholars at school, students at university, who must sit some
examination today;
Those who are leaving home for the first time today, to go to
some place that is new and strange, and people who are
beginning a new job today;
Those who have to face some interview today, the result of
which will make a very big difference to them;
Those for whom today
Work will be specially hard;
Temptation will be specially strong;
People will be specially difficult.

Bless all such people, and bless me. Grant that they and I may
be so strengthened and guided that we may come to the end
of the day with no mistakes and with no regrets: through Jesus
Christ my Lord. AMEN.

O God, I thank you for the things which I have discovered today:
For any new thing which I know now which I did not know
this morning;
For anything that has been added to my store of knowledge and
of experience;
For books that I have read and places that I have seen:
I thank you, O God.

I thank you for all the people I have discovered today:
For the friends I have known for long;
For new acquaintances whom I have made;
For people I met who have the same interests as I have, and to
    whom it was a joy to talk:
I thank you, O God.

I thank you specially for people whom I did not like and whom
    now for the first time I am beginning to understand.

Amidst all the changes of life I thank you for Jesus who is always
    the same, yesterday, today and for ever.

Hear this my evening thanksgiving, and help me to try to deserve
    it all a little better: through Jesus Christ my Lord.   AMEN.

DAILY READING

Luke 10:38–42

Now it came to pass, as they went, that he entered into a certain
village: and a certain woman named Martha received him into her
house. And she had a sister called Mary, which also sat at Jesus'
feet, and heard his word. But Martha was cumbered about much
serving, and came to him, and said, Lord, dost thou not care that
my sister hath left me to serve alone? bid her therefore that she
help me. And Jesus answered and said unto her, Martha, Martha,
thou art careful and troubled about many things: But one thing
is needful: and Mary hath chosen that good part, which shall not
be taken away from her.

FORTY-EIGHTH DAY

O God, bless all those who have very responsible jobs to do today:

Teachers who mould the minds and lives of boys and girls;
Doctors and surgeons whose skill makes people well again
   and eases their pain;
Lawyers who interpret the law, policemen who enforce the
   law, judges who administer justice;
Those in whose employment and control there are many
   workers, and whose decisions affect many lives;
Those on the roads, on the railways, at sea, and in the air,
   in whose hands are the lives and the safety of those who
   travel and journey;
Scientists who control decisions and discover powers which
   can bring life and death;
Statemen whose decisions affect the welfare of the nations
   and of the world;
Preachers who tell the story of Jesus in this land and in
   lands across the sea;
Parents to whom there has been given the privilege and the
   responsibility of a child.

Help them and support them in their work, and help me today
   to do well every task, however humble, which is given me to
   do: through Jesus Christ my Lord. AMEN.

IN THE EVENING

O God, forgive me for all today's mistakes.

When I look back, I think of
   The things I would do much better, if I had the chance to do
   them again;

The people to whom I would be so much kinder and so much more courteous, if I could meet them again;

The things that I wish I had not done, and the words that I wish I had not spoken;

The things I failed to do, and the chance to do which may never come back again;

The fine impulses which I would turn into action, if I had today again.

O God, give me sleep tonight; and in the days to come give me strength and grace to do what I know I ought to do, and to live in the way I know I ought to live: through Jesus Christ my Lord. AMEN.

DAILY READING

Psalm 136:1–5, 23–6

O Give thanks unto the Lord; for he is good: for his mercy endureth for ever.

O give thanks unto the God of gods: for his mercy endureth for ever.

O give thanks to the Lord of lords: for his mercy endureth for ever.

To him who alone doeth great wonders: for his mercy endureth for ever.

To him that by wisdom made the heavens: for his mercy endureth for ever.

Who remembered us in our low estate: for his mercy endureth for ever.

And hath redeemed us from our enemies: for his mercy endureth for ever.

Who giveth food to all flesh: for his mercy endureth for ever.

O give thanks unto the God of heaven: for his mercy endureth for ever.

FORTY-NINTH DAY

O God, my Father, give me patience all through today.

Give me patience with my work,
    so that I may work at a job until I finish it or get it right,
    no matter how difficult or how boring it may be.

Give me patience with people,
    so that I will not become irritated or annoyed, and so that I
    may never lose my temper with them.

Give me patience with life,
    so that I may not give up hope when hopes are long in
    coming true;
    so that I may accept disappointment without bitterness and
    delay without complaint.

Hear this my morning prayer for your love's sake. AMEN.

O God, as I lay myself down to rest tonight, I pray for all those
    who do not like the night;

Bless little children who are afraid of the dark.

Bless those in illness and in pain, for whom the night hours are
    very slow and very long.

Bless those who are lonely, and who in the stillness of the night
    feel their loneliness all the more.

Bless those who are sad, and who in the night time miss someone
    who is gone from them more than at any other time.

Bless those who are away from home in hospitals and in
    infirmaries, in journeyings and in distant places.

Bless those who are worried, and whose thoughts will not let them
    sleep.

O God, give me tonight a heart content and a mind at rest, so that I may sleep in peace and rise in strength: through Jesus Christ my Lord. AMEN.

John 10:7–11

Then said Jesus unto them again, Verily, verily, I say unto you, I am the door of the sheep. All that ever came before me are thieves and robbers: but the sheep did not hear them. I am the door: by me if any man enter in, he shall be saved, and shall go in and out, and find pasture. The thief cometh not, but for to steal, and to kill, and to destroy: I am come that they might have life, and that they might have it more abundantly. I am the good shepherd: the good shepherd giveth his life for the sheep.

FIFTIETH DAY

O God, grant that today
  I may not disappoint any friend;
  I may not grieve any loved one;
  I may not fail anyone to whom I have a duty.
  I may not shame myself.

Grant that today
  I may do my work with honesty and fidelity;
  I may take my pleasure in happiness and purity.

Grant that today
  I may lead no one astray;
  I may not make goodness and faith harder for anyone.

Help me today to be a help and example to all, and to bring
  strength and encouragement, wherever I may be: through Jesus
  Christ my Lord.   AMEN.

IN THE EVENING

O God, at the end of the day it is not so much the things that
  I have done which worry me as the things which I have not
  done.

Forgive me for the tasks into which I did not put my best, for work
  that was shoddy, and for workmanship of which any true
  craftsman would be ashamed.

Forgive me for the things I did not do, and for the help I did not
  give.

Forgive me for the word of praise and the word of thanks I did
  not speak:

Forgive me for my failure in courtesy and in graciousness to those with whom I live and work.

Help me each day to do better, so that each night I may have fewer regrets: through Jesus Christ my Lord. AMEN.

DAILY READING

Isaiah 6:1–8

In the year that King Uzziah died I saw also the Lord sitting upon a throne, high and lifted up, and his train filled the temple. Above it stood the seraphims: each one had six wings; with twain he covered his face, and with twain he did fly. And one cried unto another, and said, Holy, holy, holy, is the Lord of hosts: the whole earth is full of his glory. And the posts of the door moved at the voice of him that cried, and the house was filled with smoke. Then said I, Woe is me! for I am undone; because I am a man of unclean lips, and I dwell in the midst of a people of unclean lips: for mine eyes have seen the King, the Lord of hosts. Then flew one of the seraphims unto me, having a live coal in his hand, which he had taken with the tongs from off the altar: and he laid it upon my mouth, and said, Lo, this hath touched thy lips; and thine iniquity is taken away, and thy sin purged. Also I heard the voice of the Lord, saying Whom shall I send, and who will go for us? Then said I, Here am I; send me.

FIFTY-FIRST DAY

In the morning

O God, help me today and every day to use life as you would have me to use it.

Help me to use whatever gifts and whatever strength I have to help others, and to make a useful contribution to the life and the work of the world, wherever I am.

Help me to use whatever money I have, not selfishly, but generously.

Help me to use my time wisely in honest work; help me to use my spare time, not altogether selfishly, and not altogether for my own pleasure, but to do something in it for others.

Help me to use my mind to get new knowledge and to improve myself; help me never to stop learning, and not to be entirely taken up with light and frivolous things.

Help me to use today in such a way that in it I may improve myself, help others and please you: through Jesus Christ my Lord. AMEN.

In the evening

O God, when I sit and think at the end of the day, I realize how unsatisfactory I am.

So often I do not give my employers my best work.

So often I only make use of my home, and I am more disobliging and more discourteous to those who love me most than to anyone else.

So often I expect far more from my friends than I am prepared to give to them.

So often I find pleasure in things in which I shouldn't.

So often I allow thoughts and pictures to come into my mind, and feelings to come into my heart, which should never be allowed to find an entry there.

So often I refuse to give my church the help and the service I could well give, even if it does mean giving up something of my time or money.

So often I shirk work, evade decisions, refuse duties, and run away from responsibilities.

Forgive me, O God. Help me to try harder and to do better. Give me your strength to do the things which I cannot do myself. This I ask for Jesus' sake. AMEN.

DAILY READING

2 Corinthians 5: 17–21

Therefore if any man be in Christ, he is a new creature: old things are passed away; behold, all things are become new. And all things are of God, who hath reconciled us to himself by Jesus Christ, and hath given to us the ministry of reconciliation; To wit, that God was in Christ, reconciling the world unto himself, not imputing their trespasses unto them; and hath committed unto us the word of reconciliation. Now then we are ambassadors for Christ, as though God did beseech you by us: we pray you in Christ's stead, be ye reconciled to God. For he hath made him to be sin for us, who knew no sin; that we might be made the righteousness of God in him.

FIFTY-SECOND DAY

In the morning

O God, this morning, I have come into the quietness and stillness of your presence to begin the day, so that out of this moment I may take with me a quiet serenity which will last me through the rough and tumble of this day's life.

I have come to find wisdom,
    so that today I may not make any foolish mistakes.

I have come to find peace,
    so that nothing may worry or upset me all through today.

I have come to find love,
    so that all through today nothing may make me bitter or unforgiving or unkind.

I have come to begin the day with you, to continue it with you, and to end it with you, so that it will be a day which will have in it nothing to regret.

Hear this my morning prayer for Jesus' sake. AMEN.

In the evening

O God, I started out today with all kinds of high hopes and resolutions, but it has just been another of these days.

I have been just as easily irritated and annoyed as ever I was.

I have been just as easily worried and flustered and upset as ever I was.

I have been just as impatient with people, just as quick in temper and tongue as ever I was.

I have been no kinder, no more considerate, no more like Jesus.

O God, it would be easy to make excuses, to put the blame on others, to say that it was not all my fault. But I don't want to say that, because it would not really be true. All I want to say is: Forgive me, help me not to be discouraged, and not to give up the battle for goodness, and help me to do better tomorrow.

All this I ask for your love's sake. AMEN.

DAILY READING

Isaiah 53: 1–6

Who hath believed our report? and to whom is the arm of the Lord revealed? For he shall grow up before him as a tender plant, and as a root out of a dry ground: he hath no form nor comeliness; and when we shall see him, there is no beauty that we should desire him. He is despised and rejected of men, a man of sorrows, and acquainted with grief: and we hid as it were our faces from him; he was despised, and we esteemed him not. Surely he hath borne our griefs, and carried our sorrows: yet we did esteem him stricken, smitten of God, and afflicted. But he was wounded for our transgressions, he was bruised for our iniquities: the chastisement of our peace was upon him; and with his stripes we are healed. All we like sheep have gone astray; we have turned every one to his own way; and the Lord hath laid on him the iniquity of us all.

FIFTY-THIRD DAY

O God, you know me, and you know that I don't want to go out at all today.

I am tired before I start. There are people I don't want to meet; there are jobs I don't want to do. There are tasks which I will have to do, and I am not nearly as well prepared for them as I ought to be.

I would much rather stay at home, or run away from it all. But I can't do that, and I know I can't do that. I know quite well life has got to go on, no matter how I feel about it.

Lord Jesus, come with me, and help me to feel you beside me all day, so that I will not only get grimly through today, but that I may know the joy of living with you.

This I ask for your love's sake. AMEN.

O God, bless all my friends and my loved ones tonight.

Bless those whose lives are interwoven with mine, and without whom life could never be the same. Bless those to whom I owe my comfort, and without whom life would be very lonely.

Bless the one to whom I have given my heart to keep, and who has given me his/her heart to keep, and keep us for ever loyal, for ever loving, and for ever true to one another.

Bless my absent friends and loved ones, from whom for a time I am separated. Guard them, guide them, protect them, and grant that we may soon meet again.

I know that all for whom I am praying are also praying for me.

Help me just now to feel very near to them, and not only to them, but even to those whom I have loved and lost awhile, and who have gone to be with you.

Hear this my prayer for your love's sake. AMEN.

DAILY READING

1 Corinthians 3: 18–23

Let no man deceive himself. If any man among you seemeth to be wise in this world, let him become a fool, that he may be wise. For the wisdom of this world is foolishness with God. For it is written, He taketh the wise in their own craftiness. And again, The Lord knoweth the thoughts of the wise, that they are vain. Therefore let no man glory in men. For all things are yours; whether Paul, or Apollos, or Cephas, or the world, or life, or death, or things present, or things to come; all are yours; And ye are Christ's; and Christ is God's.

FIFTY-FOURTH DAY

O God, my Father, make me more appreciative of others.

Help me never to fail to say thanks for everything that is done for me, and never to take anything for granted, just because it comes to me unfailingly every day.

Help me always to be ready to speak a word of praise, whenever a word of praise is possible – and sometimes even when it is not possible.

Help me to be quick to notice things. Help me to be quick to see when someone is depressed and discouraged and unhappy. Help me to be quick to see it when someone is lonely and shy and is left out of things.

O Lord Jesus, all through today help me to see people with your eyes.

This I ask for your love's sake.   AMEN.

IN THE EVENING

Forgive me, O God, for all the trouble I have caused today.

Forgive me
　　if I made a nuisance of myself by being stupidly obstinate, or needlessly obstructive, or foolishly fussy.

Forgive me
　　if I have caused other people trouble by keeping them waiting for me, or by being late with my work, or by failing to keep a promise.

Forgive me
　　if I have annoyed others by trying to be funny at the wrong time, by making jokes about the wrong things, or by being cross, irritable, bad-tempered, discourteous.

Forgive me
if I could see no point of view but my own, or if I was hard
to work with, or difficult to live with.

Tonight, O God, forgive me. Tomorrow is another day; help me
to make a better job of it than I did of today.

This I ask for your love's sake. AMEN.

Daily reading

Isaiah 55: 6–11

Seek ye the Lord while he may be found, call ye upon him while
he is near: let the wicked forsake his way, and the unrighteous
man his thoughts: and let him return unto the Lord, and he will
have mercy upon him: and to our God, for he will abundantly
pardon. For my thoughts are not your thoughts, neither are your
ways my ways, saith the Lord. For as the heavens are higher than
the earth, so are my ways higher than your ways, and my thoughts
than your thoughts. For as the rain cometh down, and the snow
from heaven, and returneth not thither, but watereth the earth, and
maketh it bring forth and bud, that it may give seed to the sower,
and bread to the eater: So shall my word be that goeth forth out
of my mouth: it shall not return unto me void, but it shall
accomplish that which I please, and it shall prosper in the thing
whereto I sent it.

FIFTY-FIFTH DAY

O God, so help me today that nothing may make me lose my temper.

So help me that nothing may make me lose my serenity, that I may be proof alike against the big blows and the petty pinpricks of life.

So help me that nothing may make me lose my patience either with things or with people.

So help me that I may not get flustered or excited, but that I may take things easily and just as they come.

So help me to work that I may do things when they ought to be done, and as they ought to be done, so that there will be no last-minute rush today.

So help me that nothing may make me take offence or differ in bitterness with anyone today.

Today, O God, garrison my heart with your peace and equip my life with your strength.

This I ask for your love's sake.   AMEN.

In the evening

Forgive me, O God,
   if I have behaved today as if I was the only person who was busy, and as if I was the only person who had a lot to do.

Forgive me
   if I have behaved as if I was the only person for whom things were difficult and hard, and as if life was unkinder to me than to anyone else.

Forgive me
> if I have behaved as if I was the only person who was misjudged or misunderstood, and as if I was the only person who ever got a raw deal.

Forgive me for magnifying my troubles and for forgetting my blessings.
Help me from now on to get things in their right proportions by thinking far more of others and far less of myself.

This I ask for your love's sake.   AMEN.

DAILY READING

1 Corinthians 15: 53–8

For this corruptible must put on incorruption, and this mortal must put on immortality. So when this corruptible shall have put on incorruption, and this mortal shall have put on immortality, then shall be brought to pass the saying that is written, Death is swallowed up in victory. O death, where is thy sting? O grave, where is thy victory? The sting of death is sin; and the strength of sin is the law. But thanks be to God, which giveth us the victory through our Lord Jesus Christ. Therefore, my beloved brethren, be ye steadfast, unmoveable, always abounding in the work of the Lord, forasmuch as ye know that your labour is not in vain in the Lord.

FIFTY-SIXTH DAY

O God, my Father, give me today
Courage, to do the things I am afraid to do;
Conscientiousness, to do the things I do not want to do;
Grace to get alongside the people I do not like and who do not
like me.

Grant that even in the dull routine of the day's work I may find
a thrill, because I remember that I am doing it with you, so
that even the uninteresting things may become interesting, and
so that even things which seem not to matter may become
important.

Help me to be happy all through today, and to make others happy
too.

This I ask for Jesus' sake. AMEN.

O God, I thank you for today.

I thank you
that I was able to do the work which earns the pay to support
myself and those whom I love and who are dependent on me.

I thank you
for the people I met, and whose company I enjoyed.

I thank you
for any temptation you made me able to overcome;
for any new thing which I have learned;
for any useful thing I was able to do;
for anyone I know better, and to whom I have come closer today.

Help me now to go to sleep with a quiet mind, and to wake
tomorrow glad to meet another day: through Jesus Christ my
Lord.   AMEN.

Jeremiah 31: 31–4

Behold the days come, saith the Lord, that I will make a new
covenant with the house of Israel, and with the house of Judah:
Not according to the covenant that I made with their fathers in
the day that I took them by the hand to bring them out of the
land of Egypt; which my covenant they brake, although I was an
husband unto them, saith the Lord: But this shall be the covenant
that I will make with the house of Israel: After those days, saith
the Lord, I will put my law in their inward parts, and write it in
their hearts; and will be their God, and they shall be my people.
And they shall teach no more every man his neighbour, and every
man his brother, saying, Know the Lord: for they shall all know
me, from the least of them unto the greatest of them, saith the
Lord: for I will forgive their iniquity, and I will remember their
sin no more.

FIFTY-SEVENTH DAY

I thank you, O God, for health and strength to go out and to do my work; and I remember before you those who cannot go out to work today.

I remember
Those who are ill and in pain at home and in the hospitals and the infirmaries and nursing-homes;
Those who are helpless and paralysed;
Those whose nerves and minds have collapsed under the strain of living;
Those who are slowly recovering from a long illness.

I remember
Those who are old, and whose day's work is done, and who are feeling useless;
Those who are in disgrace;
Those who are unemployed, and who have no work to do, and who are worried about what is to happen to their homes and to their loved ones.

Bless all the people who are like that. And, even if my work is dull, or worrying, or hard, or badly paid, or unappreciated, help me to remember how fortunate I am to have the health and strength to do it, and help me not to forget to be grateful to you.

This I ask for Jesus' sake.   AMEN.

O God, help me tonight to relax in body and in mind.

Take from me the tension which makes rest impossible.

Take from me the worries which fill my mind with thoughts which destroy sleep.

Take from me the fears which lurk at the back of my mind, which come to haunt me when work is laid aside, and when there is too much time to think.

Help me tonight really and truly to cast my care upon you, really and truly to feel the everlasting arms underneath and about me.

Help me to sleep tonight, not just the sleep of tiredness, but the sleep of peace; through Jesus Christ my Lord. AMEN.

DAILY READING

2 Corinthians 12: 7–10

And lest I should be exalted above measure through the abundance of the revelations, there was given to me a thorn in the flesh, the messenger of Satan to buffet me, lest I should be exalted above measure. For this thing I besought the Lord thrice, that it might depart from me. And he said unto me, My grace is sufficient for thee: for my strength is made perfect in weakness. Most gladly therefore will I rather glory in my infirmities, that the power of Christ may rest upon me. Therefore I take pleasure in infirmities, in reproaches, in necessities, in persecutions, in distresses for Christ's sake: for when I am weak, then am I strong.

FIFTY-EIGHTH DAY

O God, give me the things which will make me able to live well
today.

Give me
  A sense of proportion,
    That I may see what is important and what is not important,
    and that I may not get all hot and bothered about things
    which do not matter;

  A sense of humour,
    that I may learn to laugh,
    and especially to laugh at myself, and not to take myself
    too seriously;

  A sense of responsibility,
    that I may look on each task as something which I am
    doing for the general good and for you.

Give me
  A new sensitiveness of spirit,
    that I may see when I am hurting people,
    and that I may not blindly and thoughtlessly trample on
    the feelings of others.

Give me, too, a continual awareness of the presence of Jesus, that
  I may do nothing which it would grieve him to see, and nothing
  which it would hurt him to hear.

This I ask for your love's sake.   AMEN.

IN THE EVENING

O God, I thank you for today.

I thank you for any lovely thing that I have seen or experienced.

I thank you for anything which happened to me which made me feel that life is really and truly worth living.

I thank you for all the laughter which was in today.

I thank you, too, for any moment in which I saw the seriousness and the meaning of life.

I thank you very specially for those I love, and for those who love me, and for all the difference it has made to me to know them, and for all the happiness it brings to me to be with them.

O God, my Father, forgive me for anything in today which has vexed others, which has shamed myself, which has disappointed my friends, or which has grieved you.

Give me the sense of being forgiven, that I may lay me down to sleep in peace: through Jesus Christ my Lord. AMEN.

DAILY READING

Joel 2:28–32

And it shall come to pass afterward, that I will pour out my spirit upon all flesh: and your sons and your daughters shall prophesy, your old men shall dream dreams, your young men see visions: And also upon the servants and upon the handmaids in those days will I pour out my spirit. And I will shew wonders in the heavens and in the earth, blood, and fire, and pillars of smoke. The sun shall be turned into darkness, and the moon into blood, before the great and the terrible day of the Lord come. And it shall come to pass, that whosoever shall call on the name of the Lord shall be delivered: for in mount Zion and in Jerusalem shall be deliverance, as the Lord hath said, and in the remnant whom the Lord shall call.

FIFTY-NINTH DAY

O God, all through today make me quicker to praise than to criticize.

Help me never to forget to thank people for anything that they do for me.

Make me always ready to speak a word of praise and of appreciation.

Grant that I may take no service for granted, and that I may allow no help to pass unnoticed.

Make me quick to notice when people are upset or depressed, and give me the ability to speak the word which will help and cheer them.

All through today help me to think far less of myself and far more of others, and so to find my own happiness in making others happy.

This I ask for Jesus' sake.   AMEN.

In the evening

Before I sleep tonight, I want to say a prayer for all the people – known to me and unknown to me – for whom this has been a special day of gladness or of grief, of trouble or of joy.

Bless all the homes in which today life has ended or life has begun.

Bless all the homes in which a child has been born, and take special care of the mother and the father and the little baby.

Bless those who have been married today, and grant that this may be the beginning for them of many years of loyalty and love.

Bless all homes where there has been joy or heartbreak, where there has been happy news of success or sorrowful news of failure, homes to which someone has brought honour and homes to which someone has brought disgrace.

Be very near to any home in which anyone is tempted to do some disgraceful and dishonourable and evil thing, and lay your hand upon his/her shoulder and restrain them from it.

Be in every home to comfort, to encourage, to guide, to restrain; and grant to them all to feel your presence and to know your love: through Jesus Christ my Lord.   AMEN.

DAILY READING

Galatians 6:1–5

Brethren, if a man be overtaken in a fault, ye which are spiritual, restore such a one in the spirit of meekness; considering thyself, lest thou also be tempted. Bear ye one another's burdens, and so fulfil the law of Christ. For if a man thinks himself to be something, when he is nothing, he deceiveth himself. But let every man prove his own work, and then shall he have rejoicing in himself alone, and not in another. For every man shall bear his own burden.

SIXTIETH DAY

IN THE MORNING

O God, I know that there are certain dangers which are always threatening me.

Keep me from taking people and all that they do for me for granted, and help me to show them how much I value them, and how much I appreciate all that they do for me.

Keep me from allowing myself to become satisfied with less and less, from lowering my standards, from forgetting my ideals as the days go on.

Keep me from taking sin less and less seriously, from allowing myself things which once I would have refused, from accepting as inevitable things which once would have shocked me.

Help me to walk looking unto Jesus, that I may see all things in the light of his life and of his Cross, so that I may strive to be always on the upward way.

This I ask for your love's sake. AMEN.

IN THE EVENING

O God, I thank you for today and for your help all through today.

There were things which I thought I would never be able to do, but with your help I managed to do them.

There were things of which I was frightened as I looked forward to them,
but with your help I found them not so terrible after all.

I thank you for the pleasure I found in the company of people whom up to now I thought uninteresting, or whom up to now I did not like.

I thank you that life is just as full of unexpected joys as it is of unexpected sorrows.

I thank you for the friends who grow dearer to me every day, and without whom life would never be the same.

I thank you for the people who have given me the generous love which I have done so little to deserve.

Help me to fall asleep tonight counting my blessings.

Hear this my prayer for Jesus' sake.   AMEN.

DAILY READING

Micah 6:6–8

Wherewith shall I come before the Lord, and bow myself before the high God? shall I come before him with burnt offerings, with calves of a year old? Will the Lord be pleased with thousands of rams, or with ten thousand rivers of oil? shall I give my firstborn for my transgression, the fruit of my body for the sin of my soul? He hath showed thee, O man, what is good; and what doth the Lord require of thee, but to do justly, and to love mercy, and to walk humbly with thy God?

SIXTY-FIRST DAY

O God, my Father, I thank you that this morning I am able to rise and to go to my work.

I thank you that I can move and walk, and see and hear, and think with my mind and work with my hands.

As I think of the health which I enjoy, I remember those who are blind and deaf, lame and helpless and bedridden, those who have lost their reason and whose minds are darkened and whose senses are gone.

I remember those who long to work but who are unemployed, whose talents and gifts and skills are wasting in an idleness which they hate.

Help me, O God, to live today in such a way that I may show my gratitude for all the gifts and blessings you have given me: through Jesus Christ my Lord.   AMEN.

IN THE EVENING

This morning, O God, I thanked you that I was able to rise from sleep and to go out to my work. It is good to go out, but it is still better to come home.

I thank you for keeping me safe today on the busy streets, and on my journeys to and from my work.

I thank you for any temptation which you made me able to conquer today.

I thank you that I was able to do the work which I was given to do.

I thank you for everyone who helped me and who was kind to me today.

I am sorry if I did any of my work badly, or if I hurt or disappointed anyone.

Now guard and keep me while I sleep, and waken me strengthened and refreshed tomorrow morning: through Jesus Christ my Lord.   AMEN.

DAILY READING

Hebrews 4:12–16

For the word of God is quick, and powerful, and sharper than any two-edged sword, piercing even to the dividing asunder of soul and spirit, and of the joints and marrow, and is a discerner of the thoughts and intents of the heart. Neither is there any creature that is not manifest in his sight: but all things are naked and opened unto the eyes of him with whom we have to do. Seeing then that we have a great high priest, that is passed into the heavens, Jesus the Son of God, let us hold fast our profession. For we have not a high priest which cannot be touched with the feeling of our infirmities; but was in all points tempted like as we are, yet without sin. Let us therefore come boldly unto the throne of grace, that we may obtain mercy, and find grace to help in time of need.

SIXTY-SECOND DAY

O God, it is you who have given me another day of life. Unless you help me, I know that this day will go all wrong.

Control my tongue.
Keep me from saying things which make trouble, and from involving myself in arguments which only make bad situations worse and which get nowhere.

Control my thoughts.
Shut the door of my mind against all envious and jealous thoughts; shut it against all bitter and resentful thoughts; shut it against all ugly and unclean thoughts.

Help me to live today in purity, in humility and in love.

All through today grant that no wrong thought may enter my mind and no wrong word come from my mouth: through Jesus Christ my Lord. AMEN.

IN THE EVENING

O God, my Father, tonight in the quiet time I have many people in my mind and in my heart.

Those I love:
Help me never to hurt or to disappoint them, and never to drift apart from them. Bless them and keep them safe.

My friends:
Help me never to be too selfish and too demanding with my friends; never to try to make use of them; always to try to do something to enrich their lives, as I wish that they may enrich mine.

The people with whom I work:
　　Make me easy to work with. Help me never to make the work of others harder by dodging or shirking the work I ought to be doing. Help me never to be needlessly slow to learn, or impatiently unwilling to show others how to do things, or to help them to do them.

All people in pain, in sadness, in loneliness, in trouble, in disgrace:
　　Help those who cannot help themselves, and bless those for whom their fellow men and women can do little to comfort or to support.
Bless me, and make me for ever sure of your love and your care.

This I ask for your love's sake.　AMEN.

DAILY READING

Exodus 20:1–7

And God spake all these words, saying, I am the Lord thy God, which have brought thee out of the land of Egypt, out of the house of bondage. Thou shalt have no other gods before me. Thou shalt not make unto thee any graven image, or any likeness of any thing that is in heaven above, or that is in the earth beneath, or that is in the water under the earth: thou shalt not bow down thyself to them, nor serve them: for I the Lord thy God am a jealous God, visiting the iniquity of the fathers upon the children unto the third and fourth generation of them that hate me; And shewing mercy unto thousands of them that love me, and keep my commandments. Thou shalt not take the name of the Lord thy God in vain; for the Lord will not hold him guiltless that taketh his name in vain.

SIXTY-THIRD DAY

In the Morning

O God, I will meet all kinds of people today; help me to help them all.

If I meet any who are sad,
    help me to comfort them, even if I can do no more than say a word of sympathy and shake their hand.

If I meet any who are depressed,
    help me to cheer them up, and to send them on their way happier because they met me.

If I meet any who are tempted,
    help me to help them to resist temptation by showing them an example, or by speaking a gentle word of warning to them.

If I meet any who are worried,
    help me to ease their anxiety as far as I can.

If I meet any who are overworked,
    help me to lend them a hand, if I possibly can, even if it means extra work for me, and even if I have to go a long way out of my way to do so.

If I meet any who are disgruntled and discontented,
    help me to help them to feel that things are not as bad as they think they are.

If I meet any who are happy,
    help me to share in their joy, and never to grudge it to them.

Make me able to enter into the mind and heart of all whom I meet today, and to bring joy and happiness wherever I go; through Jesus Christ my Lord.   AMEN.

O God, you know how I feel, and you know that tonight I am so tired that I can hardly stay awake to pray.

But, before I go to sleep, I must say thank you for today and I must ask your forgiveness for everything in it that was not right.

Help me now to fall asleep thinking about you, and to waken tomorrow to live for you.

This I ask for your love's sake. AMEN.

DAILY READING

Exodus 20:8–17

Remember the sabbath day, to keep it holy. Six days shalt thou labour, and do all thy work; But the seventh day is the sabbath of the Lord thy God: in it thou shalt not do any work, thou, nor thy son, nor thy daughter, thy manservant, nor thy maidservant, nor thy cattle, nor thy stranger that is within thy gates; For in six days the Lord made heaven and earth, the sea, and all that in them is, and rested on the seventh day: wherefore the Lord blessed the sabbath day, and hallowed it. Honour thy father and thy mother: that thy days may be long upon the land which the Lord thy God giveth thee. Thou shalt not kill. Thou shalt not commit adultery. Thou shalt not steal. Thou shalt not bear false witness against thy neighbour. Thou shalt not covet thy neighbour's house, thou shalt not covet thy neighbour's wife, nor his manservant, nor his maidservant, nor his ox, nor his ass, nor any thing that is thy neighbour's.

SIXTY-FOURTH DAY

Help me, O God, today,
  To shirk no duty that I should face,
  or word that I should speak.

  To avoid no person whom I ought to meet,
  or any decision which I ought to take.

  To postpone no task that I ought to do,
  nor to delay the answer to any request to which I should
    respond.

Help me
  To do each thing as it comes to me,
  And to do it faithfully, wisely and well.

Keep me alike
  From delaying the things I ought to do,
  And from rushing into the things, about which I ought to think
    before I act.

All through today grant me the wisdom which will keep me from
  all mistakes and save me from all regrets: through Jesus Christ
  my Lord. AMEN.

Thank you, O God, for making me able to do my work today, and
  for bringing me back home at evening time.

Thank you for the times today when you guided me to do what
  I ought to do, and when you strengthened me to resist the
  temptation to do what I ought not to do.

Thank you for anyone who made me able to help today, and for
  anyone to whom I have come closer.

Thank you for those who have helped me today, for those who have cheered me when I was depressed, for anyone who went out of the way to help me, for anyone who made me feel that after meeting him or her life was better than I thought.

Help me to sleep well tonight and to work well tomorrow: through Jesus Christ my Lord. AMEN.

DAILY READING

Luke 10: 25–8

And, behold, a certain lawyer stood up, and tempted him, saying, Master, what shall I do to inherit eternal life? He said unto him, What is written in the law? how readest thou? And he answering said, Thou shalt love the Lord thy God with all thy heart, and with all thy soul, and with all thy strength, and with all thy mind; and thy neighbour as thyself. And he said unto him, Thou hast answered right: this do, and thou shalt live.

SIXTY-FIFTH DAY

Give me, O God, all through today a strong sense of duty,
  so that I will not be able to shirk any task,
  to evade any decision,
  or to avoid any responsibility.

Help me to do my duty to myself,
  so that I will never lose my self-respect.

Help me to do my duty to others,
  so that I may be among my fellow men and women as one who
  serves.

Help me to do my duty to you,
  by giving myself to you body, soul and spirit,
  so that you can use me as you wish.

At the same time give me joy in all things, so that duty may not
  be a grim and joyless thing, but so that I may do everything
  as unto you.

This I ask for your love's sake. AMEN.

IN THE EVENING

O God, you are the God of peace, and I am a worrier. Take away
  my worry and give me some of your peace.

Help me not to waste my time worrying about things about which
  there is nothing to be done, but help me to accept them, and
  to make the best of them, and to overcome them.

Help me not to worry about things which I myself can mend, but
  to do something about them, even if it means a great effort, and
  even if it means that which is still more difficult – the

confessing of my error and the humbling of my pride.

Help me not to worry about the past. Although I am a sinner, help me to know and to remember that I am a forgiven sinner.

Help me not to worry about the future, but to know that I will never be tried above what I am able to bear.

Help me tonight to sleep in peace, and to waken tomorrow sure that I can face life, and all that life can demand from me, and all that life can do to me.

Hear this my prayer for Jesus' sake.   AMEN.

DAILY READING

I Corinthians 13:1–7

Though I speak with the tongues of men and of angels, and have not charity, I am become as sounding brass, or a tinkling cymbal. And though I have the gift of prophecy, and understand all mysteries, and all knowledge; and though I have all faith, so that I could remove mountains, and have not charity, I am nothing. And though I bestow all my goods to feed the poor, and though I give my body to be burned, and have not charity, it profiteth me nothing. Charity suffereth long, and is kind; charity envieth not; charity vaunteth not itself, is not puffed up, Doth not behave itself unseemly, seeketh not her own, is not easily provoked, thinketh no evil; Rejoiceth not in iniquity, but rejoiceth in the truth; Beareth all things, believeth all things, hopeth all things, endureth all things.

SIXTY-SIXTH DAY

O God, as this day begins for me, I want to remember before you
those for whom it will be hard and sad and difficult.

Bless those
Who have no work to do, and for whom the hours will be
empty;
Who today will have to watch a loved one pass from this life,
or lay a dear one to rest;
Who will go out to sadness and come home to loneliness;
Who will be stricken with sudden illness;
Who have to undergo an operation today
or who must spend it waiting for one;
Who will receive bad news;
To whom this day will bring disappointment and heartbreak.

Grant that all in sorrow, in difficulty, and in hardship may find
in you a refuge and strength, and a very present help in their
trouble.

This I ask through Jesus Christ my Lord. AMEN.

IN THE EVENING

Take from me tonight, O God,
The worries which would keep me from sleeping;
The tension which would keep me from relaxing;
The envies and the jealousies and the wrong memories,
which would make my heart bitter.

Forgive me for the things which I regret and for which I am sorry
now; and help me here and now to make up my mind to take
the first step to try to put things right tomorrow with anyone
whom I have hurt or wronged, or anyone with whom I finished
today at variance.

Help me tonight to sleep in peace, sure of your love and care surrounding me; and grant that tomorrow I may waken with my mind clear, with my body refreshed, and with my heart at peace with everyone and with you: through Jesus Christ my Lord. AMEN.

DAILY READING

I Corinthians 13:8–13

Charity never faileth: but whether there be prophecies, they shall fail; whether there be tongues, they shall cease; whether there be knowledge, it shall vanish away. For we know in part, and we prophesy in part. But when that which is perfect is come, then that which is in part shall be done away. When I was a child, I spake as a child, I understood as a child, I thought as a child: but when I became a man, I put away childish things. For now we see through a glass darkly; but then face to face: now I know in part; but then shall I know even as also I am known. And now abideth faith, hope, charity, these three; but the greatest of these is charity.

SIXTY-SEVENTH DAY

IN THE MORNING

O God, help me to make today a perfect day, a day at the end
of which I will have nothing to regret.

Help me
  To do my work as well as it can possibly be done;
  To treat everyone with perfect courtesy and kindness;
  To conquer every temptation and to say no to everything
    that is wrong.

Help me
  Not to annoy anyone else and not to allow myself to become
    annoyed;
  Not to lose my temper and not to do things which will make
    others lose theirs;
  Not to do anything that is foolish or thoughtless, cruel or
    unkind.

Help me
  To be cheerful and kind;
  To be brave and strong;
  To be pure and true.
This I ask for your love's sake.   AMEN.

IN THE EVENING

O God, this morning I set out with such good resolutions and
  with such high intentions to make this a perfect day – but it
  didn't work out that way.
  I am sorry for all the time that I have wasted;
  I am sorry for all the people at whom I snapped;
  I am sorry that I did silly things, when I wasn't thinking
    what I was doing.

There are so many things which I said and did today for which I am sorry now. I am sorry that I was needlessly annoying, bad-tempered and unkind.

Help me before I go to sleep to feel that you understand how difficult it is, and to feel that you have forgiven me. And help me to do better tomorrow, and never to give up trying: through Jesus Christ my Lord.   AMEN.

DAILY READING

Matthew 5:43–8

Ye have heard that it hath been said, Thou shalt love thy neighbour, and hate thine enemy. But I say unto you, Love your enemies, bless them that curse you, do good to them that hate you, and pray for them which despitefully use you, and persecute you; That ye may be the children of your Father which is in heaven: for he maketh his sun to rise on the evil and on the good, and sendeth rain on the just and on the unjust. For if ye love them which love you, what reward have ye? do not even the publicans the same? And if ye salute your brethren only, what do ye more than others? do not even the publicans so? Be ye therefore perfect, even as your Father which is in heaven is perfect.

SIXTY-EIGHTH DAY

In the morning

O God, help me this morning to count my blessings before I start on the day.

I thank you that I have a job to go to and work to do.

I thank you that I have the health and the strength and the skill to do it.

I thank you for my home, and for those who are very near and dear to me.

I thank you for the friends whom I will meet today, as I travel, at my work, at my meals, and when my work is done.

I thank you for everything in which I will find pleasure today, for work, for games, for books, for pictures, for films, for plays, for music, for dancing, for talks with my friends, and for times with those who are more than friends, and whom I love.

I thank you for Jesus, and for the promise that he is always with me.

Help me in that promise to find my inspiration to goodness, and my protection from sin.

Hear this my prayer for your love's sake.   AMEN.

In the evening

O God, before I sleep tonight, I want to bring to you in my prayer those whom I know who specially need your help.

Bless those in sickness, in illness, and in pain. Give them the cheerfulness, the serenity, the faith which will help them to get well.

Bless those who are sad. Comfort them; take away the ache of their loneliness, and help them to find comfort in going on.

Bless those who are worried. Help them to find the peace of mind which comes from the certainty that they will never be tested beyond what they can bear.

Bless those who are tempted. Give them grace to resist; and give your warning to those who are foolishly playing with fire.

Bless those who are far from home and far from friends, and protect them in body, mind and spirit.

Bless all those who are praying for me tonight as I am praying for them.

Hear this my prayer for your love's sake.   AMEN.

DAILY READING

John 13:31–5

Therefore, when he was gone out, Jesus said, Now is the Son of man glorified, and God is glorified in him. If God be glorified in him, God shall also glorify him in himself, and shall straightway glorify him. Little children, yet a little while I am with you. Ye shall seek me: and as I said unto the Jews, Whither I go, ye cannot come; so now I say to you. A new commandment I give unto you, That ye love one another; as I have loved you, that ye also love one another. By this shall all men know that ye are my disciples, if ye have love one to another.

SIXTY-NINTH DAY

O God, keep me from the things which are bound to cause trouble.

Keep me from
  The self-will which unreasonably insists on its own way;
  The self-conceit which cannot stand the slightest criticism;
  The touchiness which sees offence where no offence was ever
    intended.

Keep me from
  The tale-bearing tongue;
  From all delight in malicious gossip;
  From repeating that which was said in confidence.

Keep me from
  The eyes which can see nothing but faults;
  The mind which can think only the worst;
  The tongue whose delight it is to criticize.

Help me
  To think with kindness;
  To speak with courtesy;
  To act in love.

Help me to live as one who has been with Jesus.

This I ask for your love's sake.   AMEN.

In the evening

O God, thank you for today.

Thank you
  For happy things which came to me quite unexpectedly;
  For things which turned out to be not nearly so bad as I
    expected;

For difficult things which became quite manageable when I
faced up to them.

Forgive me for the things I did not do,
   For the letter which is still not answered;
   For the promise which is still not kept;
   For the decision which is still delayed;
   For the habit which is still not given up.

Make me honest enough to see myself as I am, and humble enough
   to seek from you the help I need, so that what I cannot do,
   your grace may do for me: through Jesus Christ my Lord.

AMEN.

DAILY READING

Proverbs 3:13–18

Happy is the man that findeth wisdom, and the man that getteth
understanding. For the merchandise of it is better than the
merchandise of silver, and the gain thereof than fine gold. She is
more precious than rubies; and all the things thou canst desire
are not to be compared unto her. Length of days is in her right
hand; and in her left hand riches and honour. Her ways are ways
of pleasantness, and all her paths are peace. She is a tree of life
to them that lay hold upon her; and happy is every one that
retaineth her.

SEVENTIETH DAY

O God, grant that all through today I may never find any request
    for help a nuisance.

Help me never to find a child a nuisance,
    when he wants me to help him with his lessons,
    or play with him in his games.

Help me never to find a sick person a nuisance,
    if he would like me to spend some time with him,
    or do some service for him.

Help me never to find someone who is old a nuisance,
    even if he is critical of youth,
    settled immovably in his ways,
    demanding of attention.

Help me never to find a nuisance anyone who asks me,
    To show him how to do things,
    To help him in his work;
    To listen to his troubles.

Grant, O God, that I may neither be too immersed in work or
    too fond of my own pleasure, that I may never be too busy and
    never too tired, to help those who need help, even if they are
    the kind of people who get on my nerves and whom I
    instinctively dislike.

Help me to help, not only when it is pleasant to help, but when
    help is difficult and when I don't want to give it: through Jesus
    Christ my Lord.　AMEN.

O God, the thing that hurts me most to remember at night is how
    I hurt others through the day.

Forgive me
  For cruelly and mercilessly criticizing others;
  For laughing at people;
  For thinking people fools, and for letting them see that I
    thought they were.

Forgive me
  For any request that I refused;
  For any sympathy that I did not give;
  For any disloyalty which brought pain to the heart of a friend.

O God, I know that so often I have not treated others as I would
  wish them to treat me; I have treated them as I would hate to
  be treated.
Forgive me and help me to be kinder tomorrow: through Jesus
  Christ my Lord.   AMEN.

DAILY READING

Philippians 2:5–11

Let this mind be in you, which was also in Christ Jesus; Who, being in the form of God, thought it not robbery to be equal with God: But made himself of no reputation, and took upon him the form of a servant, and was made in the likeness of men; And being found in fashion as a man, he humbled himself, and became obedient unto death, even the death of the cross. Wherefore God also hath highly exalted him, and given him a name which is above every name: That at the name of Jesus every knee should bow, of things in heaven, and things in earth, and things under the earth; And that every tongue should confess that Jesus Christ is Lord, to the glory of God the Father.

PRAYERS WITH BIBLE READINGS FOR FESTIVAL DAYS

THE FIRST DAY OF THE YEAR

IN THE MORNING

Eternal and everblessed God, who makes all things new, we thank you that today you have allowed us to begin a new year.

Here in your presence we make our resolutions for the days to come.

We resolve to be faithful and true to those who love us, and loyal to those who are our friends, so that we may never bring worry to their minds or distress to their hearts.

We resolve to live in forgiveness and in kindness, that, like our Master, we may go about ever doing good.

We resolve to live in diligence and in effort, that we may use to the full the gifts and the talents which you have given us.

We resolve to live in goodness and in purity, that we ourselves may resist temptation, and that we may be a strength to others who are tempted.

We resolve to live in sympathy and in gentleness, that we may bring comfort to the sorrowing and understanding to the perplexed.

We resolve to live in serenity and in self-control, that no anger and no passion may disturb our own peace and the peace of others.

We resolve to live in full obedience and in perfect love to you, that in doing your will we may find our peace.

O God, our Father, who has given us grace to make our resolutions, grant us also strength to keep them all this year: through Jesus Christ our Lord.   AMEN.

IN THE EVENING

O God, our Father, already we have come to the end of the first day of this new year.

Help us never to forget how quickly time passes on its way, and so help us to use every moment of it to the utmost.

Help us to remember that opportunities come, and that often they never return, and so help us to seize them when they come.

Help us to remember that we never know when time will end for us, and so make us at all times to have all things ready to depart and to go to you.

O God, our Father, even this one day has shown us how hard it is to keep the resolutions which we have made. Help us to remember that without you we can do nothing, and so help us to walk each step with you, that in your protecting presence life may be safe from sin. This we ask for your love's sake. AMEN.

DAILY READING

Matthew 28:16-20

Then the eleven disciples went away into Galilee, into a mountain where Jesus had appointed them. And when they saw him, they worshipped him: but some doubted. And Jesus came and spake unto them, saying, All power is given unto me in heaven and in earth. Go ye therefore, and teach all nations, baptizing them in the name of the Father, and of the Son, and of the Holy Ghost: Teaching them to observe all things whatsoever I have commanded you: and, low, I am with you alway, even unto the end of the world. AMEN.

GOOD FRIDAY

IN THE MORNING

O God, our Father, we thank you this day that you so loved the
   world that you gave your only Son for us and for all mankind.
We give you thanks this day for Jesus Christ, our blessed Lord,
   and for his death upon the Cross.

That he was obedient unto death, even the death of the Cross;
That he loved us and gave himself for us;
That he came to seek and to save that which was lost;
That he gave his life a ransom for many, a ransom for us:
We give you thanks this day, O God.

Greater love hath no man than this, that a man lay down his life
   for his friends. Help us this day to remember, and never again
   to forget, the love of him who laid down his life for us.

> *O wondrous love! to bleed and die,*
> *To bear the Cross and shame,*
> *That guilty sinners, such as I,*
> *Might plead Thy gracious Name!*

Hear this our prayer, for your love's sake.   AMEN.

IN THE EVENING

O Lord Jesus Christ, who did say, I, if I be lifted up from the earth
   will draw all men unto me, fix our eyes this night upon your
   Cross.

Help us in your Cross to see the lengths to which man's sin will
   go. Help us in the Cross to see that sin is enmity to you, that
   sin is the destroyer of all beauty, and the enemy of all loveliness.
Help us in the Cross to see the lengths to which your love will
   go, that you loved us so much that you kept nothing back.

Help us in the Cross to see the horror of sin, and to depart for
ever from it.

Help us in the Cross to see the wonder of love, and to surrender
for ever to it.

This we ask for your love's sake.   AMEN.

John 19: 14–18

And it was the preparation of the passover, and about the sixth
hour: and Pilate saith unto the Jews, Behold your King! But they
cried out, Away with him, away with him, crucify him. Pilate saith
unto them, Shall I crucify your King? The chief priests answered,
We have no king but Caesar. Then delivered he him therefore unto
them to be crucified. And they took Jesus, and led him away. And
he bearing his cross went forth into a place called the place of
a skull, which is called in the Hebrew Golgotha: Where they
crucified him, and two other with him, on either side one, and
Jesus in the midst.

EASTER DAY

O Lord Jesus Christ, who upon this day did conquer death and rise from the dead, and who are alive for ever more, help us never to forget your Risen Presence for ever with us.

Help us to remember,
That you are with us in every time of perplexity to guide and to direct;
That you are with us in every time of sorrow to comfort and to console;
That you are with us in every time of temptation to strengthen and to inspire;
That you are with us in every time of loneliness to cheer and to befriend;
That you are with us even in death to bring us through the waters to the glory on the other side.

Make us to be certain that there is nothing in time or in eternity which can separate us from you, so that in your presence we may meet life with gallantry and death without fear.

This we ask for your love's sake. AMEN.

In the evening

O Lord Jesus Christ, forgive us for the times when we have forgotten your Risen Presence for ever with us.

Forgive us for times when we failed in some task because we did not ask your help.
Forgive us for times when we fell to some temptation because we tried to meet it by ourselves.
Forgive us for times when we were afraid, because we thought that we were alone in the dark.

Forgive us for times when we were driven to despair, because we were trying to fight the battle in our own unaided strength.

Forgive us for times when we said and did things which now we are ashamed to remember that you heard and you saw.

Forgive us for times when death seemed very terrible, and the loss of loved ones beyond all bearing, because we forgot that you had conquered death.

Make us this night again to hear you say: Lo, I am with you alway even unto the end of the world, and in that promise grant to us to find courage and strength to meet all things undismayed.

This we ask for your love's sake.   AMEN.

DAILY READING

Luke 24:1–6

Now upon the first day of the week, very early in the morning, they came unto the sepulchre, bringing the spices which they had prepared, and certain others with them. And they found the stone rolled away from the sepulchre. And they entered in, and found not the body of the Lord Jesus. And it came to pass, as they were much perplexed thereabout, behold, two men stood by them in shining garments: And as they were afraid, and bowed down their faces to the earth, they said unto them, Why seek ye the living among the dead? He is not here, but is risen.

WHITSUNDAY

IN THE MORNING

Eternal and everblessed God, who upon this day did send your
Spirit with power upon your people, let your Spirit be upon us.

Let your Spirit be in our minds, to guide our thoughts towards
the truth.

Let your Spirit be in our hearts, to cleanse them from every evil
and unclean desire.

Let your Spirit be upon our lips, to preserve us from all wrong
speaking, and to help us by our words to commend you to
others.

Let your Spirit be upon our eyes, that they may find no delight
in looking on forbidden things, but that they may be fixed on
Jesus.

Let your Spirit be upon our hands that they may be faithful in
work and eager in service.

Let your Spirit be upon our whole lives, that they may be strong
with your power, wise with your wisdom, and beautiful with
your love: through Jesus Christ our Lord.   AMEN.

IN THE EVENING

Eternal and everblessed God, who has sent your Spirit to be our
teacher and our guide, help us never to be afraid to follow where
your Spirit leads.

Help us never to be afraid of new truth, but always to open our
minds to your Spirit's teaching.

Help us never to be afraid of courageous action, but ever to act
without fear as your Spirit prompts.

Help us never to be afraid of the criticism or the persecution of
men, but ever to be certain that it will be given to us through

---

your Spirit what we must do and what we must say to defend the faith.

Let your Spirit move within the hearts of all men, that he may inspire them to discover truth, to spread abroad beauty, and to live in love.

And grant to us ourselves to yield ourselves wholly to your Spirit, that you may be able to equip us for your work, and to use us in your service: through Jesus Christ our Lord.   AMEN.

DAILY READING

John 14: 15–17, 25–7

If ye love me, keep my commandments. And I will pray the Father, and he shall give you another Comforter, that he may abide with you for ever; Even the Spirit of truth; whom the world cannot receive, because it seeth him not, neither knoweth him: but ye know him; for he dwelleth with you, and shall be in you. These things have I spoken unto you, being yet present with you. But the Comforter, which is the Holy Ghost, whom the Father will send in my name, he shall teach you all things, and bring all things to your remembrance, whatsoever I have said unto you. Peace I leave with you, my peace I give unto you: not as the world giveth, give I unto you. Let not your heart be troubled, neither let it be afraid.

ALL SAINTS' DAY

Eternal and everblessed God, we remember this day the unseen
cloud of witnesses who compass us about. We remember the
blessed dead who do rest from their labours, and whose works
do follow them. And we give you thanks for all of them.

For parents who gave us life; who tended and cared for us in years
when we were helpless to help ourselves; who toiled and
sacrificed to give to us our chance in life; at whose knees we
learned to pray, and from whose lips we first heard the name
of Jesus:
  We give you thanks, O God.

For teachers who taught us;
For ministers of your Gospel who instructed us in your truth and
in your faith;
For all those who have been an example to us of what life should
be;
For those whose influence on us will never cease, and whose
names will never depart from our memory;
  We give you thanks, O God.

For the saints, the prophets and the martyrs;
For those who lived and died for the faith;
And, above all else, for Jesus, the captain of our salvation and the
author and finisher of our faith;
  We give you thanks, O God.

Grant to us in our day and generation to walk worthily of the
heritage into which we have entered: through Jesus Christ our
Lord.   AMEN.

O God, our Father, we remember this day all those whom we have loved and lost awhile.

We remember those whom you did take to yourself full of years and honour.
We remember those whom in the midtime you did call.
We remember those for whom the flower of life never had time to blossom.
We remember all those whose earthly course is ended, and who are in your nearer presence.

Take from us all sadness, and teach us to sorrow not as others who have no hope.
Turn our thoughts from the darkness of death to the life eternal; and grant to us the sure certainty that one day we shall be reunited in your presence with those whom we have loved.

This we ask for your love's sake.   AMEN.

DAILY READING

Hebrews 11:39–12:2

And these all, having obtained a good report through faith, received not the promise: God having provided some better thing for us, that they without us should not be made perfect. Wherefore seeing we also are compassed about with so great a cloud of witnesses, let us lay aside every weight, and the sin which doth so easily beset us, and let us run with patience the race that is set before us, Looking unto Jesus the author and finisher of our faith; who for the joy that was set before him endured the cross, despising the shame, and is set down at the right hand of the throne of God.

CHRISTMAS DAY

In the morning

O God, our Father, we thank you for Christmas time, and for all
that it means to us.

We thank you that, when Jesus, your Son, came into this world,
he came into a humble home.
We thank you that he had to grow up and to learn like any other
boy.
We thank you that he did a good day's work, when he grew to
manhood, as the carpenter in the village shop in Nazareth.
We thank you that he was tempted and tired, hungry and sad,
just as we are.
We thank you that he was one with his brethren in all things, that
he truly shared this life with its struggles and its toils, its
sorrows and its joys, its trials and its temptations.
We thank you that he knew what it is to live in a home circle,
just as we do; to earn his living, just as we do; to know
friendship and to know the failure of friends, just as we know it.
We thank you for the service of his life; the love of his death; and
the power of his Resurrection.

Grant, O God, that, when he comes to us, he may not find that
there is no room in our hearts for him; but grant that this
Christmas day he may enter into our hearts and abide there
for ever more.

Hear this our prayer, for your love's sake.   AMEN.

In the evening

O God, our Father, we thank you for the happiness of this
Christmas Day.

For the presents we have received; for the happiness we have

enjoyed; for the meals we have eaten together, the games we have played together, the talk we have had together,
We thank you, O God.

We thank you for the peace and goodwill which have been amongst us all today. Grant that they may not be something which lasts only for today; but grant that we may take the Christmas joy and the Christmas fellowship with us into all the ordinary days of life.

Now at evening time we specially remember those for whom Christmas has not been a happy time. Bless those to whom sorrow came, and for whom it was all the sorer, because it came at the time when everyone else was so happy. Bless those who have no friends, no homes, no family circle, no one to remember them; and be with them in their loneliness to comfort and cheer them. O God, we thank you for today; help us to try to deserve all our happiness a little more. Through Jesus Christ our Lord. AMEN.

DAILY READING

Luke 2:11–14

For unto you is born this day in the city of David a Saviour, which is Christ the Lord. And this shall be a sign unto you; Ye shall find the babe wrapped in swaddling clothes, lying in a manger. And suddenly there was with the angel a multitude of the heavenly host praising God, and saying, Glory to God in the highest, and on earth peace, good will toward men.

THE LAST DAY OF THE YEAR

O God, our Father, today we are remembering all the ways by
which you have brought us to this present hour, and we thank
you for every step.

We thank you for every experience which has come to us, because
we know that in it and through it all you have been loving us
with an everlasting love.

For gladness and for grief; for sorrow and for joy; for laughter and
for tears; for silence and for song;
    We give you thanks, O God.

That you have kept us in our going out and our coming in;
That you have enabled us to do our work, and to earn our living;
That you have brought us in safety to this present hour:
    We give you thanks, O God.

For any new things that we have learned, and for any new
experiences through which we have passed;
If we can do our work a little better, and if we know life a little
better;
For friends who are still closer to us, and for loved ones who are
still more dear:
    We give you thanks, O God.

And today, as we remember the passing years, we thank you most
of all for Jesus Christ, the same yesterday, today and for ever.
Help us to go on, certain that, as you have blessed the past,
so the future is also for ever in your hands: through Jesus Christ
our Lord. AMEN.

O God, our Father, tonight we are looking back across the year which is passing from us now.

There is so much for which we need forgiveness.

For the time we have wasted; for the opportunities we have neglected; for the strength we have given to the wrong things; for all the mistakes we have made:
Forgive us, O God.

There is so much for which we ought to give you thanks.
For health and for strength; for protection in the time of danger; for healing in the time of illness; for upholding in the day of sorrow; for daily light and daily leading:
We thank you, O God.

Bless those for whom this has been a happy year, and make them to give the thanks to you. Bless those for whom this has been a sad year, and help them still to face the future with steady eyes. And help us in the year to come so to live that at the end of it we shall not only be one year older, but that we shall also be one year nearer you. This we ask for your love's sake. AMEN.

DAILY READING

Psalm 90:12 and 17

So teach us to number our days, that we may apply our hearts unto wisdom.
And let the beauty of the Lord our God be upon us: and establish thou the work of our hands upon us; yea, the work of our hands establish thou it.

Prayers for
Special Occasions

PRAYERS FOR
SPECIAL OCCASIONS
IN THE HOME

When a child is born

O God, our Father, we give you thanks for this little child who has come to us from you. Bless *him** now and through all the days of his life.

Protect him in the days of his helplessness; bring him in safety through childhood's dangers; and grant that he may grow to manhood, and do a good day's work, and witness for you.

Help us his parents so to love him and so to train him that we shall not fail in the trust which you have given us, and that, even as you have given him to us, we may give him back in dedication to you: through Jesus Christ our Lord. AMEN.

When a child goes to school

O God, our Father, our child is going to school for the first time today; and we cannot help being anxious at this first step away from home.

Keep *him* safe from all that would hurt *him* in body or harm *him* in mind.

Help *him* to be happy at school, and to know the joy of learning and playing together with other boys and girls.

Help *him* to learn well that *he* may grow up to stand on *his* own feet, to earn *his* own living, and to serve you and *his* fellow men and women: through Jesus Christ our Lord. AMEN.

When there is a marriage in the family

O God, our Father, whose greatest gift is love, bless . . . and . . . who today within your presence will take each other in

* *him* denotes *or her*, etc.

marriage. We thank you that they have found such love and faith and trust in each other that they wish to take each other to have and to hold all the days of their life. Let nothing ever come between them, but throughout all the chances and the changes of life keep them forever loving and forever true. Keep them safe from illness, from poverty, from all trouble which would hurt them in any way. But, if any trial does come to them, grant that it may only drive them closer together and closer to you. Grant to them through all their days the perfect love which many waters cannot quench and which is stronger than even death itself: through Jesus Christ our Lord. AMEN.

IN THE TIME OF ILLNESS

O God, our Father, bless and help . . . in the illness which has come upon *him*.

Give *him* courage and patience, endurance and cheerfulness to bear all weakness and all pain; and give *him* the mind at rest, which will make *his* recovery all the quicker.

Give to all doctors, surgeons and nurses who attend *him* skill in their hands, wisdom in their minds, and gentleness and sympathy in their hearts.

Help us not to worry too much, but to leave our loved one in the hands of wise and skilful men who have the gift of healing, and in your hands.

Lord Jesus, come to us and to our loved one this day and at this time, and show us that your healing touch has never lost its ancient power. This we ask for your love's sake. AMEN.

IN THE TIME OF SORROW

O God, our Father, we know that you are afflicted in all our afflictions; and in our sorrow we come to you today that you may give to us the comfort which you alone can give.

Make us to be sure that in perfect wisdom, perfect love, and perfect power you are working ever for the best.

Make us sure that a Father's hand will never cause his child a needless tear.

Make us so sure of your love that we will be able to accept even that which we cannot understand.

Help us today to be thinking not of the darkness of death, but of the splendour of the life everlasting, for ever in your presence and for ever with you.

Help us still to face life with grace and gallantry; and help us to find courage to go on in the memory that the best tribute we can pay to our loved one is not the tribute of tears, but the constant memory that another has been added to the unseen cloud of witnesses who compass us about.

Comfort and uphold us, strengthen and support us, until we also come to the green pastures which are beside the still waters, and until we meet again those whom we have loved and lost awhile: through Jesus Christ our Lord. AMEN.

WHEN BAD NEWS COMES

O God, our Father, whatever comes to us make us able to stand on our feet, and to face it with steady eyes. Help us to be sure that we will never be tried above that which we are able to bear. Help us to be sure that your grace is sufficient to make even our weakness able to face and to conquer anything that can come to us. Make us sure that in the valley of the deep dark shadow you are there to comfort and to support; and that when we pass through the waters you are there to hold us up, and to bring us through them to the other side: through Jesus Christ our Lord. AMEN.

WHEN GOOD NEWS COMES

O God, my Father, who has portioned out all my life for me, I thank you for the good news which has come to me today. I thank you that you have given me success; that my hope is realized, that my dream has come true, and that my ambition is fulfilled. Keep me today and in the days to come from all pride and from all self-conceit. Help me to remember that without you I can do nothing. So keep me all my days in humility and in gratitude to you: through Jesus Christ our Lord. AMEN.

In the Hour of Temptation

Lord Jesus, you know what temptation is like. You know how strongly the wrong thing fascinates me, and how much the forbidden thing attracts me. Lord Jesus, help me not to fall.

Help me to remember my own self-respect, and to remember that I cannot do a thing like this.

Help me to think of those who love me, and to know that I dare not bring disappointment and heartbreak to them.

Help me to remember the unseen cloud of witnesses who compass me about, and to know that I cannot grieve those who have passed on, but who are for ever near.

Help me to remember your presence, and in your presence to find my safety. This I ask for your love's sake. AMEN.

In the Time of Decision

O God, you know that today I must make a decision which is going to affect my whole life. Help me to choose the right way. Grant me your guidance, and with it grant me the humble obedience to accept it. Help me not to choose what I want to do, but what you wish me to do. Grant that I may not be swayed by fear or by hope of gain, by selfish love of ease or comfort or by personal ambition, by the desire to escape or the longing for prestige. Help me today in humble obedience to say to you: 'Lord, what will you have me to do?' and then to await your guidance, and to accept your leading. Hear this my prayer, and send me an answer so clear that I cannot mistake it. This I ask for your love's sake. AMEN.

In the Time of Journeying and Separation

O God, our Father, beyond whose love and care we cannot drift, bless . . . in *his* journeying today. Bring *him* in safety to *his* journey's end; and let no ill befall *him* in body, mind or spirit. Grant that, when we are separated from each other, we may ever remember that, though we are absent from one another, we are still present with you. And keep us true and faithful to each other until we meet again: through Jesus Christ our Lord.
AMEN.

O God, our Father, we thank you for this time of rest from our daily work and our daily business.

We thank you for time to spend with our family and in the circle of those most dear.

We thank you for the open road, and the hills and the seashore, and for the clean wind upon our faces.

We thank you for games to play, for new places to see, new people to meet, new things to do.

Grant that the days of our holiday may refresh us in body and in mind, so that we may come back to work the better, because we rested awhile: through Jesus Christ our Lord. AMEN.

IN THE TIME OF DISAPPOINTMENT

O God, my Father, you know the disappointment which has come to me today; and you know that that which I wished for and longed for has not come to me. Keep me from feeling resentful and bitter. Keep me from feeling ill-used and from developing a grudge against life.

Keep me from being jealous and envious of those who have entered into that which was denied to me. Keep me from wasting my time in vain regrets, and from making myself wretched and making others unhappy.

Help me to count the blessings that I have. Help me to serve you and to serve my fellow men and women with my whole heart in whatsoever place life has set me, and in whatsoever work has been given me to do: through Jesus Christ our Lord.

AMEN.

AFTER A QUARREL

O God, you know that today I have broken your commandment of love, and that I have parted with my neighbour in anger. Even if I have been wronged and insulted, teach me how to forgive. Even if I was right, help me to make the first approach and to take the first step to putting things right again. Keep me from foolish pride and from nursing my foolish anger. Help me to be looking at Jesus, that in him I may see the example of how to forgive, and that in him I may find the will and the power to forgive: this I ask for your love's sake. AMEN.

IN A TIME OF WORRY AND ANXIETY

O God, you know how worried and anxious I am about . . .
Help me to be sensible, and to see that worrying about things does not make them any better.
Help me to be trustful, and to do all that I can, and then to leave the rest to you.
Help me to be sure that nothing can happen to me through which you can not bring me in safety; and that nothing can separate me from your love.
Help me to lose my anxiety in the certainty that the everlasting arms are underneath me and about me; and give me something of the peace which the world cannot give, and cannot ever take away: through Jesus Christ our Lord. AMEN.

WHEN WE COME TO THE END OF OUR WORKING DAYS

O God, today I am going out to my work for the last time. I thank you for all the years of work which you have enabled me to do. I thank you for the strenuous working years of my life, and now I thank you that you have given to me a time for rest. Help me to lay down my work gratefully and graciously and not grudgingly and resentfully, and not to be envious and jealous of the younger people who are stepping into my place. In the days to come keep me from rusting in idleness. Keep me still interested in life; still of service to others; still finding something to do; still learning; and still happy to the very end: through Jesus Christ our Lord. AMEN.

WHEN WE HAVE MADE MISTAKES AND FALLEN TO TEMPTATION

O God, my Father, you know that today I have fallen to temptation and that I have done wrong. I have brought shame to myself, anxiety to those who love me, and grief to you. O God, in your mercy, forgive me for Jesus' sake. Help me to be brave enough not only to confess this sin to you and to ask your forgiveness, but to ask the forgiveness of the person I have hurt and wronged and injured, and to do all I can to put things right again. Keep me from too much regret, too much remorse, and help me to rise above the error I have made and the wrong that I have done. In the days to come help me not to make the same mistake again. Give me a conscience which is quick and tender, and give me grace always to obey it. Help me to walk with Jesus that in his company I may be saved from sin and enabled to do the right. This I ask for your love's sake. AMEN.

IN TIME OF A DISASTER

O God, I remember before you those on whom at this time disaster has come.

Bless those whose dear ones have been killed, and those whose dear ones have lost their lives in seeking to save the lives of others.

Bless those who have lost their homes, and those who have seen all that they toiled for a lifetime to build up lost in an hour.

Help us always to remember those whose job it is to risk their lives to rescue others or to keep them safe – those in the fire service, in the lifeboat service, in the police service, in the mountain rescue service, in the medical service.

We will forget this disaster, but we ask you in your love always to remember those who will never forget because life for them can never be the same again.

This we ask for your love's sake. AMEN.

AT THE TIME OF A
HOLIDAY TRAGEDY

———

O God, Father of all comfort and God of all grace,

Bless those for whom the joy of holiday time has turned to tragedy.

Those who have lost dear ones in accidents on the roads, on the beaches and at sea, in the hills, on the railways, in the air, by the sudden and unexpected coming of death into their family circle.

Help us to remember that there is always someone who is sad, that never morning wore to evening but some heart did break, and comfort those for whom happy days in the sunshine turned suddenly to the midnight of a broken heart.

This I ask for your love's sake. AMEN.

PRAYERS FOR ANNIVERSARIES

FOR A HAPPY ANNIVERSARY

O God, today I am happy as I look back and remember.

I thank you for that day . . . years ago which was the beginning of joy for me.

I thank you for the happy years you have given to me in my home, at my work, within my church.

I thank you for all the friends and the comrades and the loved ones with whom throughout the years my life has been intertwined.

This day, as you have commanded me, I remember all the way by which you have brought me to this present hour, and I thank you for it.

Hear this my thanksgiving through Jesus Christ my Lord.

AMEN.

FOR A SAD ANNIVERSARY

O God, today brings me memories that are sad.

Sometimes in the busy world and at my work I can forget. But you have given us hearts which are so vulnerable, and the sight of a place, a photograph, a tune, the sound of a word, and above all a day like this, sets my heart throbbing with pain again, and I feel again the blank in life which nothing can fill.

Help me not to sorrow overmuch as those who have no hope. Help me still to face life with steady eyes, remembering that the one I loved is not gone for ever, but that another has been added to the unseen cloud of witnesses who compass me about. And bring quickly the time when the memories which make me

cry will be the memories which make me smile: through Jesus
Christ my Lord. AMEN.

O God, I thank you that you have given us another year of life
together.

I thank you
For the love which grows more precious and for the bonds
which grow more close each day.

I thank you
For the happiness we have known together;
For the sorrows we have faced together;
For all the experiences of sunshine and of shadow through
which we have come to today.

I ask your forgiveness
For any disloyalty on my part;
For any times when I was difficult to live with;
For any selfishness and inconsiderateness;
For any lack of sympathy and of understanding;
For anything which spoiled even for a moment the perfect
relationship which marriage should be.

Spare us to each other to go on walking the way of life together,
and grant that for us it may be true that the best is yet to be:
through Jesus Christ my Lord. AMEN.

O God, I thank you for giving me another year of life.

I thank you for all the people who have remembered me today,
and who have sent me cards, and letters, and good wishes, and
presents.

I thank you for everything which I have been enabled by you to
do and to be in the past year.

I thank you for all the experiences of the past year:
For times of success which will always be happy memories;

For times of failure which reminded me of my own weakness
and of my need for you;
For times of joy when the sun was shining;
For times of sorrow which drove me to you.

Forgive me
For the hours I have wasted;
For the chances I failed to take;
For the opportunities I missed in the past year.

Forgive me that I have not made of life all that I might have made
of it and could have made of it; and help me in the days which
lie ahead to make this the best year yet, and in it to bring credit
to myself, happiness to my loved ones, and joy to you.

This I ask for Jesus' sake. AMEN.

WHEN WE HAVE DONE WELL

Thank you, O God, for the success which you have given me today.

Help me not to rest on my oars because I achieved something, but to work still harder, to aim still higher, to do still better.

Keep me from becoming conceited. Help me always to think, not of what I have done, but of what I still must do; not of the few things in which I have succeeded, but of the many things in which I have failed.

Help me to be happy in the joy of achievement, but save me from a boastful and a foolish pride.

This I ask for Jesus' sake.   AMEN.

WHEN WE HAVE FAILED

O God, you know how badly I have failed in the task which I attempted, and which was given me to do, and in which I so much wanted to do well.

Don't let me become too depressed and discouraged; help me to have the determination to try again and to work still harder.

Don't let me try to put the blame on everyone and on everything except myself.

Don't let me be resentful and bitter about this failure; but help me to accept both success and failure with a good grace.

Don't let me be envious and jealous of those who have succeeded where I have failed.

Don't ever let me talk about giving up and giving in; but help me to refuse to be beaten.

Help me to learn the lesson which you want me to learn even from this failure; help me to begin again, and not to make the same mistakes again.

Maybe it is hardest of all to meet the eyes of those who are disappointed in me. Help me even yet to show them that I deserve their trust and to let them see what I can do.

This I ask for your love's sake. AMEN.

FOR ONE WHO IS TIRED

O God, somehow nowadays I am always tired. I go to sleep tired and I get up still tired.

Things take longer than they used to take, and I get behind with my work, and with the things I ought to do.

I come home tired, and that makes me cross and bad-tempered and irritable and impatient with my own family and my own people.

Everything has become an effort and a labour.

O God, help me to keep going, and help me to find something of the rest which you alone can give. Refresh me with your presence, and give me back the joy of living and the thrill of working: through Jesus Christ my Lord.   AMEN.

FOR ONE WHO IS TEMPTED

O God, there are things about which I can't talk to anyone except to you. There are things in me about which no one knows except myself and you.

The things which I should not even want fascinate me. The thoughts which I should never allow into my mind, I cannot keep out.

So far I have resisted the wrong things, but I know my own weakness, and I am afraid of myself.

O God, come to me with your cleansing power, and make me able to overcome evil and to do the right.

I ask even more – fill me with such a love of you that I will not even want to sin any more.

This I ask for Jesus' sake. AMEN.

FOR ONE WHO HAS
FALLEN TO TEMPTATION

———————

O God, I know that there is nothing which I can hide from you. I can hide my failure and my shame from others, but I cannot hide them from you. You know what I have done, and you know how sorry I am for it.

I am sorry more than anything else for the way in which I have hurt and disappointed and failed those who hoped in me, and believed in me, and love me.

I have come to you to ask for your forgiveness, to ask for strength and grace and courage to face up to things, to try even yet to redeem myself.

Forgive me. Keep me from doing the same wrong thing again. Help me to live from now on in that purity and that honesty and that goodness which you alone can give, and which you alone can preserve.

Hear this my prayer for your love's sake.   AMEN.

FOR ONE WHO IS SAD

O God, I come to you for comfort.

You know how lonely I am without . . . There are so many things which keep reminding me of . . ., and of all that I have lost.

O God, keep me from living too much in the past. Keep me from living too much with memories and too little with hopes.

Keep me from being too sorry for myself. Help me to remember that I am going through what many another has gone through. Help me not to sorrow as those who have no hope.

Help me to find comfort in my work, and, because I have gone through sorrow myself, help me to help others who are in trouble. Help me to keep trying to face life with gallantry, until I meet again the loved one whom I have lost awhile.

This I ask for your love's sake. AMEN.

FOR ONE WHOSE NERVES
HAVE BROKEN DOWN

O God, I have come to the stage when I cannot face life any longer.

I get so tense that I cannot relax. Always at the back of my mind there is the fear that I will get worse than I am now.

I know that nothing can help me, unless I help myself. I cannot help myself, and so, because things have got beyond me, I come to you.

Help me to feel that you know, that you understand, and that you care.

I used to love my work, but now I am frightened of it. I used to love life, but now I am afraid of it.

Give me the peace which comes from stopping struggling and from leaving things to you. Help me really to cast myself and my burden on you. Give me the courage to face my life, myself, my work, and the world again. Help me to win this battle which I know that by myself I can only lose.

Hear this my prayer, for your love's sake.   AMEN.

FOR ONE WHO IS SELFISH

O God, in my heart of hearts, when I stop and think, I know that I am selfish.

I always want things done for me. I always want my own way. I demand from others far more than I am prepared to give. If I am honest, I have got to admit that I try to make use of people. I never think of the trouble that I give to others. I know that I am thoughtless, and I know that I am often careless of the feelings of others, that I often hurt them because I am thinking of myself and of no one else. I know that I am so often ungrateful, that I forget how much I owe to others, and that I very seldom make any attempt to repay it.

O God, make me aware, not just at odd moments, but all the time, how ugly this selfishness is. Fix before my eyes the example and the Cross of my Lord, who, though he was rich, yet for my sake became poor. Help me to dethrone self, and to enthrone him within my heart, so that I may learn from him to love others and not myself.

This I ask for your love's sake. AMEN.

FOR ONE WHO IS PROUD

O God, I know that my besetting sin is pride.

So often I find myself looking down on others, and even despising
them. I find myself thinking of my own cleverness, and of my
own triumphs and achievements. I find myself thinking that I
am sensible, and that other people are fools.

O God, take away my pride and my self-conceit.

Help me not to compare myself with other people, but to compare
myself with Jesus, so that, when I set myself in the light of his
goodness and of his beauty, I may never again be satisfied with
myself. Help me to set myself in the light of his holiness, so
I may see how unworthy, how inadequate, how ignorant I am.

And, when shame replaces pride, give me your grace, so that
through it I may find in you the things I know I need and have
not got.

Hear this my prayer, for your love's sake.   AMEN.

FOR ONE WITH A
QUICK TEMPER

O God, I know that my temper is far too quick.

I know only too well how liable I am to flare up, and to say things for which afterwards I am heartily sorry.

I know only too well that sometimes in anger I do things which in my calmer moments I would never have done.

I know that my temper upsets things at home; that it makes me difficult to work with; that it makes me lose my friends; that far too often it makes me a cause and source of trouble.

O God, help me. Help me to think before I speak. When I feel that I am going to blaze out, help me to keep quiet just for a moment or two, until I get a grip of myself again.
Help me to remember that you are listening to everything I say, and seeing everything I do.

O God, control me and my temper too.

This I ask for your love's sake. AMEN.

FOR SOMEONE
WHO PUTS THINGS OFF

O God, I know how apt I am to put things off.

Sometimes it is because I am too lazy to do them. Sometimes it is just because I am afraid to do them. Sometimes it is because I just can't make up my mind, and I shilly-shally, and can't make a decision. Sometimes it is because I say to myself that tomorrow will be time enough.

I know that I have got into this bad habit, and I know that it causes trouble for myself and for other people, and I am only too well aware that because of it things that ought to have been done have never been done – and some of them can never be done at all now.

O God, help me to do better.

Help me to remember that for all I know tomorrow may never come.

Give me resolution to make up my mind, and strength and courage to act on my decision.

Help me never to leave until tomorrow what I ought to do today; and help me within each day to do the tasks and to make the decisions which the day demands.

Hear this my prayer for your love's sake.   AMEN.

FOR ONE WHO
IS IN TOO BIG A HURRY

O God, I know that I am in far too big a hurry.

I dash at things with far too little preparation, and without thinking of the consequences of them. Far too often I speak and act without thinking. Far too often I start something without counting the cost.

I am far too impatient both with things and with people. I have never learned to wait. I try to do things as quickly as I can and not as well as I can. My life is full of sudden enthusiasms which blaze up and just as quickly die down.

The result of all this is that my life is full of things I began and never finished, and took up and never continued, and which have to be done all over again because they were done in far too big a hurry. My frantic efforts to save time just waste time in the end.

Help me to take a grip of myself. Help me to take time to think. Give me patience to wait and perseverance to continue. Help me to think of how slowly and patiently you work, and to remember that it is better to do things well than to do them quickly.

Hear this my prayer for your love's sake. AMEN.

FOR CONTENTMENT

O God, keep me from grumbling.

I am quite well aware – from experience – that there is no one harder to put up with than someone who is always complaining. Don't let me become like that. Don't let me have discontentment written all over my face, and the whine of the east wind for ever in my voice.

If I can't get my own way,
    don't let me sulk about it.

If I can't get what I want,
    help me to make the best of what I can get, and of what I have.

Don't let me become one of these people who take offence far too easily, and who go off in a huff, even when nothing unpleasant was ever intended.

Help me all day every day
    to look on the bright side of things,
    and to see the best in people.

And help me to live in the certainty that you are working all things together for good, if I have only the trust to accept them, and the patience to wait for your purposes to work out.

This I ask for your love's sake. AMEN.

THAT I MAY NOT
WASTE THE PRECIOUS
THINGS OF LIFE

O God,

Help me not to waste my time. Don't let me always be in a hurry and a fuss, but help me to go on quietly and without haste, filling every minute with the work which is given me to do.

Help me not to waste my strength. Help me to see quite clearly the things which matter and the things which don't matter. Give me a sense of proportion that I may not get all hot and bothered about things which are of no importance, and so make myself too tired and exhausted to do the things which really matter.

Help me not to waste my money. Don't let me be mean and miserly, but help me to spend wisely and to give generously, and to try to use everything I have remembering that it belongs, not to me, but to you.

Above all, help me not to waste my life. Help me to use the talents you have given me, to seize the opportunities you are sending to me, so that some day you may be able to say to me: Well done!

You are the Lord and Master of all good life; hear this my prayer and help me to live well: through Jesus Christ my Lord.

AMEN.

A SATURDAY NIGHT PRAYER

O God, you have given us your own day to worship and to rest. Bless all those who tomorrow will preach and proclaim your word.

Give them a message from you to their people. Grant that on their lips the old themes may become new, and the old story as vivid as if it had never been told before.

Give them such a love of truth that they will think of nothing but to speak it; but give them also such a love and care for their people that they will speak the truth in sympathy and in love.

Give them, as they speak,
A word of comfort
  for the sad in heart;

A word of certainty and of light
  for the seeking and the searching and the doubting mind;

A word of strength
  for those who are wrestling with temptation;

A word of grace
  for those who are very conscious of their sin.

Bless all who tomorrow will worship in your house.

Grant that their time of worship may not be a nuisance which must be endured, or a respectable convention which must be observed. Grant that they may come in joy, in faith, and in expectation; and make them very sure that none will be sent empty away.

Bless all church members who will not worship in your house tomorrow.

If they are held at home by sickness or by the care of the sick, by the care of children and of household things, by weakness or by age, because they must work even on Sunday, or because they were too sad to come, make them to know that you and we remember them. If they stayed away because they did not wish to come, make them to remember their vows and to worship as they ought.

Bless those to whom the Church is nothing, and who will never even think of coming.

If they have forgotten you, we know that you have not forgotten them; and help us to bring your lost children back into the family of the Church.

Hear this my prayer through Jesus Christ my Lord.   AMEN.

PRAYERS BEFORE
GOING TO CHURCH

———

O God, bring me to your church in the right spirit today.

Grant that in my heart there may be no bitterness to anyone, and help me to remember that I cannot be at one with you, if I am not at one with my fellow men and women.

Take from me the critical and fault-finding spirit, so that I may really and truly go to church only to worship.

Take from me the selfish and the self-centred spirit, so that I may think, not only of what I am going to get out of this service, but also of what I am going to give and to bring to it.

Bless my minister. Give him a message for his people today, and uphold and support him in the high task you have given him to do.

Grant that in church today I may seek for nothing but to hear your truth and to see Jesus.

This I ask for your love's sake.   AMEN.

O God, help me this morning to worship you in spirit and in truth.

Make me willing to listen to the truth, even if the truth hurts and condemns me.

Keep my thoughts from wandering, and help me to concentrate on listening to you.

Help me not only to listen to the prayers, and not only to repeat them, but really to share in them.

Put out of my heart every bitter and unforgiving thought which would be a barrier between me and you. Help me to remember that I cannot have your friendship, if I am out of friendship with my fellow men and women.

Help me to go to church today with no other purpose than to listen to your word to me. Take from me the critical spirit and give me the mind and heart which are ready and open to receive.

Bless the preacher; and give him a message this morning for his waiting people, and give him strength and courage, grace and winsomeness to deliver it. Grant that this morning the whole congregation may be saying: Sir, we would see Jesus.

This I ask for your love's sake.   AMEN.

A PRAYER AFTER CHURCH

O God, don't let me forget everything that I heard and felt in church today.

Don't let me think that any word of warning and rebuke was meant for other people but not for me.

Don't let me forget that moment when I really did feel that you were near and close to me.

Don't let me forget the sorrow and the regret and the repentance which in that moment I really did feel for the wrong things in life; and don't let me forget the way in which I did feel that I must, with your help, be better.

Don't let the fact that today I met Jesus and listened to your word all go for nothing.

This I ask for your love's sake.   AMEN.

BEFORE BIBLE STUDY

Prepare me in mind and heart, O God, to listen to and to receive what your word has to say to me.

Bind me in loving fellowship with this group of people with whom I study, so that we may all be able to talk with freedom, knowing that no one will misunderstand, and no one will take offence.

Guard me from the prejudices which would blind me to the truth. Keep me from reading into your word what I want to hear, and rather help me humbly to listen to what you want to say to me.

Help me to bring to the study of your word all the help that the saints and the scholars of the past and the present can give to me to help me to understand it better; and grant that I may fearlessly follow the truth wherever it may lead me.

And then, when I have learned from your word what you want me to do, give me grace and strength to go out and to do it: through Jesus Christ my Lord. AMEN.

Prayers for
Different Occupations

A CHURCH
OFFICE-BEARER'S PRAYER

O God, to whom the Church belongs, thank you for giving me a special task and a special place within it.

Help me never to think of my office in the Church as a position of honour; help me always to think of it as an opportunity of service. Help me never to think of it as a privilege without thinking of it as a responsibility. Help me never to think of it as an opportunity to rule others; help me always to think of it as an obligation to serve others. So grant that my position may never make me proud, but that it may always keep me humble.

Help me never to make trouble, but always to make peace. So help me always to speak the truth, but always to speak it in love.

Help me never to stand on the letter of the law; never to be concerned with my own rights, my own place, my own importance. Help me to remember that he who would be chief must be the servant of all.

Make me faithful in my duty to the members of this congregation, and help me always to uphold the hands of my minister in sympathy and in prayer.

And out in the world at my day's work and in my pleasure make me a good advertisement for the Church which it is my honour to serve: through Jesus Christ my Lord. AMEN.

A CHOIR MEMBER'S AND
AN ORGANIST'S PRAYER

Thank you, O God, for giving me the privilege of leading the praise of your people in your house today.

Help me always to remember that this is not an opportunity to show my talents but to serve you and your people in your house. So banish from my heart every thought of self and pride, and help me to sing and to make music only because I truly love you with my whole heart.

Help me to remember that there are those whose hearts can be reached and touched by music even more than by speech, and so help me to remember that I too have my ministry and I too today can bring someone to you.

This I ask for Jesus' sake.   AMEN.

A SUNDAY SCHOOL
TEACHER'S PRAYER

Lord Jesus, I remember that you said: Let the little children come to me, and never try to stop them. I thank you that you have honoured me by giving me the task of bringing boys and girls to you.

Help me to do this great work as it ought to be done.

Grant that I may never meet these boys and girls unprepared. Help me to remember that, if I am teaching, I must be always learning. Help me to remember that, if I am a teacher, I must never stop being a scholar.

Grant that I may wisely and lovingly combine the discipline which will make the boys and girls respect me, and the kindness which will make them love me. Help me never to lose patience and never to lose my temper, however inattentive and troublesome they may be. Help me never to stop loving them. And help me throughout the weeks to build up a relationship with them in which they will come and ask me about anything which is worrying them, sure that I will always be ready to listen to them and always ready to understand and to sympathize.

Grant that I may always respect them and be strictly honest with them, and that I may never, to save bother, tell them something which they will afterwards have to unlearn.

Help me
  To teach them to think;
  To teach them to live;
  To teach them to love.

And at all times help me to teach more by what I am than by what I say.

This I ask for your love's sake.   AMEN.

A BIBLE CLASS
LEADER'S PRAYER

O God, you have given me a very difficult job to do within your Church.

Help me never to face these young people unprepared.

Help me to be absolutely honest with them. Help me never to dodge their questions, and never to evade their problems.

Help me to try to understand them before I criticize them. Keep me from the foolishness of looking for old heads on young shoulders, and help me to remember that the ways of one generation are not the ways of another, and that things are different since I was their age.

Help me never to laugh at them, and never to lose patience with them. Help me to be wise enough to know when they need control and discipline, and when it is better to let them have their own way.

Help me to help them to think, to worship and to pray.

Help me to remember that, whether I like it or not, and whether I know it or not, they will judge the Church by me, and that this is the grave responsibility that is laid upon me.

Even if I see no result, help me not to be discouraged. Help me to remember that it takes a long time for a seed to become a tree, and help me to sow the seed and to leave its growth to you.

Grant that what I am may never undo all that I say. You have given me this part of your work to do – help me to do it well.

This I ask for your love's sake.   AMEN.

A PARSON'S PRAYER

Lord Jesus, you have very specially called me to be a fellow-worker with you.

Make me diligent in my preparation to preach, determined never to offer to you or to my people that which cost me nothing.

Make me faithful in my visitation, a shepherd who bears each one of his flock upon his heart.

Make me constant in prayer, so that I may never go out to meet people until I have met you.

Help me to meet opposition, obstruction, misunderstanding, misrepresentation with your gentleness, your love, and your forgiveness.

Help me never to lose faith and hope even when nothing seems to be happening, but help me to be content to sow the good seed and to leave the increase to you.

Help me never to lose my temper, never to speak in irritation, never to be on terms of enmity with any man.

Give me firmness and resolution to stand for what I believe to be right, yet give me sympathy and tolerance to understand the point of view of others.

Help me never to make anyone feel a nuisance when he comes to see me, and help me to suffer even fools gladly.

Make me like you, among my fellow men and women as one who serves.

This I ask for your love's sake. AMEN.

A PRAYER FOR MISSIONARIES

O God, bless all those who have gone out to bring the message of the Gospel to other lands.

I remember before you
    Those who have to endure hardship and discomfort;
    Those who have to face peril and danger;
    Those who have had to leave their families and their children behind while they went out to other lands;
    Those who have to struggle with a new language and with new ways of thought;
    Those whose health has broken down under the strain, and who have had to come home, not knowing whether they will ever be fit for their task again;
    Those who have to face constant discouragement in a situation in which no progress ever seems to be made.

Especially bless those who work in countries where new nations are being born, and where there is strife and trouble and bitterness in the birth-pangs of the new age.

Bless those who preach in the villages and the towns and the cities; those who teach in the schools and the colleges; those who work in the hospitals and among the sick; those who have laid their gifts of craftsmanship or administration on the altar of missionary service.

Help us at home never to forget them and always to pray for them. And help us to give generously of our money to their work so that it may go where we ourselves cannot go.

And bring quickly the day when the knowledge of you will cover the earth as the waters cover the sea: through Jesus Christ my Lord. AMEN.

A PRAYER FOR THOSE
WHO ARE NEWLY MARRIED

O God, we two want to begin our life together with you, and we want always to continue it with you.

Help us never to hurt and never to grieve one another.

Help us to share all our work, all our hopes, all our dreams, all our successes and all our failures, all our sorrows and all our joys. Help us to have no secrets from one another, so that we may be truly one.

Keep us always true to one another, and grant that all the years ahead may draw us ever closer to one another. Grant that nothing may ever come between us, and nothing may ever make us drift apart.

And, as we live with one another, help us to live with you, so that our love may grow perfect in your love, for you are the God whose name is love.

This we ask for your love's sake.   AMEN.

A MOTHER'S PRAYER

O God, help me always to remember that you have given to me the most important task in the world, the task of making a home.

Help me to remember this when I am tired of making beds, and washing clothes, and cooking meals, and cleaning floors, and mending clothes, and standing in shops. Help me to remember it when I am physically tired in body, and when I am weary in mind with the same things which have to be done again and again, day in and day out.

Help me never to be irritable, never to be impatient, never to be cross. Keep me always sweet. Help me to remember how much my husband and my children need me, and help me not to get annoyed when they take me for granted, and when they never seem to think of the extra work they sometimes cause me.

Help me to make this home such that the family will always be eager to come back to it, and such that, when the children grow up and go out to their own homes, they will have nothing but happy memories of the home from which they have come.

This I ask for your love's sake.   AMEN.

A FATHER'S PRAYER

O God, help me to be true to the great privilege and the great responsibility which you have given to me.

Help me to be an example and a friend to my children, and a real partner to my wife.

Don't let me get so busy with work and with outside things that I am almost a stranger in my own home, and that I take no interest in household things.

Don't let me take all that is done for me for granted, and help me to keep love alive within the home.

Keep me from habits which make the work of the house harder, and from ways which irritate and annoy, or which get on the nerves of those who live with me.

Give me health and strength and work to do, to earn a living for those who depend on me and whom I love so much; but help me to remember that love is always more important than money.

O God, you have given me the name of father; you have given me your own name; help me to be true to it.

This I ask for your love's sake.   AMEN.

A SON'S OR A DAUGHTER'S PRAYER

Thank you, O God, for the home and for the parents you have given me.

Thank you for

All the loving care which I received when I was a child and when I could not care for myself;

All that was provided for me – food and clothes and shelter – in the years before I could earn my own living and support myself;

All the opportunities of education and of learning which my parents gave to me;

All the security I have enjoyed, the door of home always open, the sympathy and the love when I was hurt or discouraged or depressed.

Thank you for all the loving care with which I have been surrounded ever since I was born.

Forgive me, if I have done anything to hurt or to grieve my parents, and, if, as I have grown older, I have drifted away from them until we are almost strangers.

or,

Thank you, if the passing of the years has made me understand my parents better, and has made me love them more, and has drawn me closer and closer to them.

Forgive me, if I have taken everything for granted, if sometimes I just made use of my home, if I took everything and gave nothing.

Forgive me, if sometimes I have been difficult to live with, irritable, rebellious, disobedient, uncommunicative, impatient of advice, angry at restraint.

Help me at least to try to do something to show my gratitude, and to try to repay the debt I owe, even if it never can be fully repaid.

Help me so to value my home, so to love my parents, so to show them that I love them, that some day, when they are gone and I look back, I may have nothing to regret.

Hear this my prayer for Jesus' sake. AMEN.

A TEACHER'S PRAYER

Lord Jesus, when you lived and worked and talked amongst men in Palestine, they called you Teacher.

Help me to remember the greatness of the work which has been given to me to do.

Help me always to remember that I work with the most precious material in the world, the mind of a child. Help me always to remember that I am making marks upon that mind which time will never rub out.

Give me patience with those who are slow to learn, and even with those who refuse to learn.

When I have to exercise discipline, help me to do so in sternness and yet in love. Keep me from the sarcastic and the biting tongue, and help me always to encourage and never to discourage those who are doing their best, even if that best is not very good.

Help me to help these children, not only to store things in their memories, but to be able to use their minds, and to think for themselves.

And amidst all the worries and the irritations and the frustrations of my job, help me to remember that the future of the nation and of the world is in my hands.

This I ask for your love's sake.   AMEN.

A DOCTOR'S PRAYER

Lord Jesus, when you were on earth, you healed all those who had need of healing.

Help me always to remember that you have honoured me by giving me the task of continuing your healing work.

Give me skill in my mind, gentleness in my hands, and sympathy in my heart.

Help me always to remember that often when people come to me, they are frightened and nervous, and help me always to try to bring to them, not only healing for their bodies, but also calm to their minds.

Make me patient yet firm with the foolish malingerer who wastes my time.

When I must tell people that there is nothing that human skill or hands can do for them, give me a wise gentleness to break the news to them.

Help me never to lose the thrill of bringing new life into the world, and never to become callous to the pathos of the parting of death.

Give me something of your skill to heal men's diseases, to ease men's pains, and to bring peace to men's troubled minds.

This I ask for your love's sake. AMEN.

A PRAYER FOR THOSE
WHO SERVE THE COMMUNITY
in town and district councils, and in Parliament,
in trade unions, and in all public service

O God, grant that in all the public work which has been given to me to do my only motive may be to serve my fellow men and women, and my only master may be my conscience.

Help me to set loyalty to the right things above all loyalty to party or to class.

Grant that the importance of my work may never make me full of my own self-importance, but rather that it may make me humbly eager to serve and to help the people whom I represent.

Give me wisdom in my mind, clearness in my thinking, truth in my speaking, and always love in my heart, so that I may try always to unite people and never to divide them.

Help me always to set the interests of the community above those of the party; the interest of the nation above the interest of the community; and faithfulness to you above everything else.

So grant that at the end of the day I may win the approval of my own conscience, the respect of men, and your Well done!
This I ask for the sake of Jesus who was among his fellow men and women as one who served. AMEN.

A PRAYER FOR
THOSE IN AUTHORITY

for masters, employers, managers, foremen, directors

O God, you have given me the great responsibility of being in authority over my fellow men and women.

Help me always to act fairly and justly; but to justice help me always to add mercy and sympathy. Help me to know when to enforce discipline and when to relax it. Help me never to be guilty of prejudice against any one or favouritism for any one.

Help me to remember that people are always more important than things, and that men are always more important than machines.

Keep me from exercising my authority in harshness or in tyranny, and keep me also from being afraid to exercise it at all, and help me by my presence and my example to make myself and those who work under me one united band of brothers.

Help me to remember that, though I am called master, I too have a Master, even Jesus Christ.

Hear this my prayer for your love's sake. AMEN.

A SCHOLAR'S PRAYER

O God, you are the source and the giver of all wisdom and of all truth. I lay no claim to the name of scholar, but life has set me in this University/College/School, where I must learn and where I must teach.

Give me diligence, perserverance, accuracy in my study, and help me to seek for truth as blind men long for light.

Give me clarity, sympathy, enthusiasm in my teaching, and grant that I may ever seek to open the minds of those whom I teach to beauty and to truth. And grant that I may never wish those whom I teach to think as I think, but that I may ever seek to teach them to think for themselves.

Grant that my life within this place of learning may not separate and isolate me from the life and work of the world of business and of trade and of industry and of commerce.

Grant that at the end of the day I may have taken a little further the torch of knowledge and of truth which was handed on to me.

This I ask for your love's sake and for your truth's sake. AMEN.

A FARMER'S OR
A GARDENER'S PRAYER

O God, I thank you for the gifts which the garden, the fields and the orchards bring to us.

I thank you for the green of the grass and the colours of the flowers, and for all the loveliness of nature which is more beautiful than the robes of kings. I thank you for all the growing things which bring food and health to men.

I thank you for the sleep of the winter, the rebirth of the spring, the golden glory of the summer, for the harvest of the autumn.

Grant that the mysterious way in which growth goes on, silently and unseen, night and day, may always make me think of you, the giver of it all.

I thank you that you gave to me the love of the soil and of all growing things, and the gift of green fingers which know nature's ways and secrets.

Help me in nature's life to see you who are the giver of all life, and to catch a glimpse of the endless life which death can never destroy: through Jesus Christ my Lord.   AMEN.

A MUSICIAN'S PRAYER

O God, I thank you for your gift to men of music.

I thank you

    For the music which tells of the sorrows of the human heart, and which can also soothe them;

    For the music which expresses human joy;

    For the music which thrills and challenges the spirit of man;

    For the music which says things which words are powerless to say.

I thank you that you gave me the ability to enjoy music and to understand it. I thank you for the ability to create it. I thank you alike for the music which makes the feet of men dance and for the music which makes the hearts of men pray.

Help me to worship and to serve you in your gift of music, and grant that I may always be ready to use this gift of mine for your service and for the joy of men: through Jesus Christ my Lord. AMEN.

A PRAYER FOR
SHOP ASSISTANTS
and for all who serve the public

Lord Jesus, you have given me the task of serving the public –
and it isn't always easy.

Help me to be patient with the time-wasting.

Help me to be courteous to the discourteous.

Help me to be forbearing to the unreasonable.

Help me to be always cheerful, always obliging, always willing to
go the extra mile in service.

Make me such that people will go away happier and smiling
because I served them today.

Hear this my prayer for your love's sake.   AMEN.

AN OFFICE-WORKER'S
PRAYER

O God, my work is with the word processor and the calculator and the ledger and the accounts and the invoices and things like that.

It isn't work that is much in the limelight or that people see very much of. I am just like a very small cog in a very big machine. But help me to remember that no machine can run well unless even the smallest part of it is doing its job.

So help me to be careful and punctual in my work. Help me to be interested in my work and to take a pride in it. Keep me from making careless mistakes which hold things up and which mean that things have to be done over again and which waste everyone's time. Help me to be willing and easy to work with.

And help me always to be courteous and cheerful so that this office will be a happier place, because I work in it: through Jesus Christ my Lord.   AMEN.

A NURSE'S PRAYER

Lord Jesus, help me to love my job, and help me to feel that I am really doing your work, and really helping you, when I look after people who are sick.

Help me at all times to have
Patience with the unreasonable, the querulous and the irritating;
Sympathy with the frightened and the nervous;
And never let me neglect those who are quiet and uncomplaining.

When people telephone or come to ask how their friends or loved ones are getting on, help me to remember how worried and anxious they are, and to do my best to help them.
Give me a steady nerve when difficult things have to be done. Make me very attentive to orders and instructions and very obedient in carrying them out; and in an emergency make me able to think for myself and to come quickly to a decision.

Give me skill; but give me gentleness.
Give me efficiency; but make me kind.
Make me firm; but make me understanding too.

Help me to study with diligence and to work with willingness; and help me to love my work and to love the people whom it is my work to help.

This I ask for your love's sake.   AMEN.

A PRAYER FOR THOSE
WHO ADMINISTER THE LAW

O God, I know that it is from you that men have learned what goodness and justice are.

Give me a mind that is fair and impartial, and give me the power to judge and to decide with wisdom and with equity.

Grant that nothing may ever make me pervert the course of justice, neither the promise of reward nor the threat of vengeance.

Grant that I may never be influenced either by the fear or the favour of men.

Make me to know that there are times when mercy is greater than justice, and when love is better than law.

Help me to help others rather to settle their disputes and differences in peace and friendship than to pursue them in bitterness and contention; and make me not only an expert in the law, but also a wise counsellor to those who come to me for help and for advice: through Jesus Christ my Lord.

AMEN.

A POLICEMAN'S PRAYER

O God, you have given me the task of maintaining law and order in this community. It is a much more dangerous and frustrating task than once it was.

Give me the courage and the resolution at all times to do my duty, and give me such a love and respect for justice that neither promise nor threat will ever make me depart from it.

Help me in a real sense to be the guardian and the friend of the whole community, a friend to the children, an example to youth, a counsellor and adviser to all good citizens.

Give me the skill and the wisdom and the strength I need to capture the evildoer and to keep him from his misdeeds. And give me at all times wisdom to know when to enforce and when to relax the letter of the law.

Help me to be a personal example of the honesty, the goodness, the justice which it is my duty to maintain; and help me to win the authority which comes from respect: through Jesus Christ my Lord.   AMEN.

A PRAYER FOR THOSE IN THE
FIRE SERVICE AND THE LIFEBOAT SERVICE
and for all those whose task it is
to rescue others

O God, you have given to me the task of rescuing those who are in trouble and in danger. Help me to find pride and pleasure in the thought that there is no greater task than the task of saving others.

Sometimes I have to risk my own life in seeking to save the life and the property of others. When I think of the perils which I must face, and when I remember those who gave their lives in facing them, help me to remember that Jesus said: Greater love hath no man than this, that a man lay down his life for his friends.

Others may have better-paid jobs, and jobs which are safer and in which the hours and the work are easier, but no one has a bigger and a more important job than I have.

Lord Jesus, you are the Saviour of the world; help, strengthen and protect me that in my own way and in my own sphere I too may be ready to risk all to save others.

This I ask for your love's sake. AMEN.

A CIVIL SERVANT'S PRAYER

O God, you have given me a share in the administration of this country. I don't hit the headlines in the newspapers; people don't know my name as they know the names of the famous politicians, and members of Parliament, and members of the government. But help me always to have the great satisfaction of knowing that they would be helpless without the ordinary routine work which I have to do, and that without it the life of the country would come to a stop. So give me joy and pride in my work, even if it is unseen.

Help me to be efficient, but not soulless.

Help me always to remember that, although I usually never see them, I am dealing with real flesh and blood people with hearts that can be hurt and minds which can be bewildered, and not with names on a schedule or numbers on a card index.

Give me courtesy, even when I have to enforce regulations which dishonest people are trying to dodge.

In all my work help me to remember that I am a human being dealing with human beings.

This I ask for your love's sake. AMEN.

A PRAYER FOR A WELFARE WORKER
OR A SOCIAL WORKER

O God, I sometimes think that I have the hardest job of all, because what I am really trying to do is to make bad people good and to make foolish people wise – and it is a hard job.

Help me
  Never to lose patience;
  Never to abandon hope;
  Never to regard anyone with loathing or contempt;
  Never to stop caring.

Help me always to love the sinner, however much I may hate the sin. And help me always to try to understand what makes people act as they do; and help me sometimes to stop and think what I would be like, if I had had as little chance as some of them have had.

Make me always
  Sympathetic to failure;
  Patient with folly;
  Firm with shiftlessness;
  Stern to cruelty;
  Resolute against those who make vice and evil easier for others.

Help me to be wise enough to know
  When to be kind and when to be stern;
  When to encourage and when to rebuke;
  When to give and when to refuse.
Above all, never let love grow cold within my heart.

Lord Jesus, you came to seek and to save that which was lost, and it is your work that I am still trying to do.

Hear this my prayer for your love's sake. AMEN.

A SOLDIER'S PRAYER

O God, you have set me under discipline. Make me not only at all times obedient to my leaders, but give me the self-discipline which will make me always obedient to the voice of conscience, and to the command of the highest that I know.

Help me always and everywhere to behave in such a way that I will be an honour and a credit to the traditions of my regiment and to the uniform and the badge which I wear.

Bless and protect those whom I love and those who love me, and, when the call of duty separates me from them, keep me true to them and them true to me.

If so it be that some day I must fight, help me to fight only to make peace, only to protect the helpless and the weak, only to support that which is just and right.

Help me at all times to fear you and to honour the Queen.

This I ask for Jesus' sake. AMEN.

A SAILOR'S PRAYER

O God, I ask you to take me into your care and protection along with all those who go down to the sea in ships.

Make me alert and wise in my duties. Make me faithful in the time of routine, and prompt to decide and courageous to act in any time of crisis.

Protect me in the dangers and the perils of the sea; and even in the storm grant that there may be peace and calm within my heart.

When I am far from home and far from loved ones and far from the country which I know, help me to be quite sure that, wherever I am, I can never drift beyond your love and care.

Take care of my loved ones in the days and weeks and months when I am separated from them, sometimes with half the world between them and me. Keep me true to them and keep them true to me, and every time that we have to part, bring us together in safety and in loyalty again.

This I ask for your love's sake.   AMEN.

AN AIRMAN'S PRAYER

O God, I thank you that I live in an age in which things that even my father never dreamed of have become commonplace.

I thank you that you have given me the power to travel higher than the clouds and faster than the wind across the sky.

Give me a fit body, a clear eye, a steady nerve and a mind able to make instant decisions.

Protect me in my journeyings, and bring me always safely to my flight's end; and help me, as I journey far above the clouds in the vast spaces of the sky, to feel your presence near: through Jesus Christ my Lord.   AMEN.

A SCIENTIST'S PRAYER

O God, give me in all my work the spirit of reverence.

As I search for the secrets of the universe,
   And as I seek to discover nature's laws,
   Help me to see behind it all your creative power and purpose.
   Help me to love nothing so much as the truth,
   And fearlessly to follow wherever truth may lead me.

Give me at all times
   The spirit of service,
   That I may think and calculate, experiment and search,
   Never for power to destroy,
   But always for power
      To lighten men's burdens;
      To feed men's hunger;
      To ease men's pain;
      To make the world a better place to live in,
      Nearer to men's hearts' desire,
      And closer to what you meant it to be.

And above all
   Give me the humility
   Which will make me,
   Not proud of what I have discovered,
   But conscious of all that I do not know,
   And which will always make me think of truth,
   Not as something I have found,
   But as something which you have given me,
   And which must be used
   As you would have it to be used.

This I ask for your love's sake. AMEN.

AN ATHLETE'S PRAYER

I thank you, O God, for giving me a body which is specially fit and strong, and for making me able to use it well.

In my training
Help me never to shirk the discipline which I know that I need and that I ought to accept.

In my leisure and in my pleasure
Help me never to allow myself any indulgence which would make me less fit than I ought to be.

When I compete with others
Help me, win or lose, to play fair. When I win, keep me from boasting; when I lose, keep me from making excuses. Keep me from being conceited when I succeed, and from being sulky when I fail. And help me always with good will to congratulate a better man who beat me.

Help me so to live that I will always have a healthy body and a healthy mind.

This I ask for your love's sake. AMEN.

A MOTORIST'S PRAYER

O God, every time I drive my car, help me to remember that I am responsible, not only for my own life, but also for the lives of others.

Give me patience, when progress is annoyingly and frustratingly slow, so that I may not endanger my own life and the lives of others by taking a chance to save a minute or two.

Give me courtesy, so that I may think of the other driver as well as of myself.

Keep me always alert, and give me wisdom to know when it is time to stop and rest.

Help me never to indulge in any habit or in any pleasure which would make me a danger to others on the road.

Help me to do everything that one person can do to make life safer on the roads on which I drive: through Jesus Christ my Lord.

AMEN.

A TRADESMAN'S OR
A CRAFTSMAN'S PRAYER

O God, it is you who gave me skill in my hands. You gave me the ability to make wood and metals and the materials out of which things are made obedient to my hands and to my will.

Give me pride in my work. Give me such self-respect that I will always be ashamed to turn out any inferior bit of workmanship or a shoddily done job.

Make me at all times absolutely honest in my work, more concerned to do a job as well as it can be done than with reckoning how much I will get out of it, or how long it will take me to do it.

Help me to work, not to satisfy the clock, but to satisfy my own conscience. Lord Jesus, you were a craftsman in Nazareth, working with the tools of your trade; make me as good a worker as you were.

This I ask for your love's sake. AMEN.

A PRAYER FOR A WRITER,

*an author, or a journalist, for all whose craft it is
to use words which many will hear or read*

O God, you gave me the gift and the responsibility of using words. Help me in all my writing and my speaking to be the servant of goodness, of beauty and of truth. Help me never to write or to say anything which would injure another's innocence or take another's faith away.

Help me never to write or say anything which would make that which is wrong more attractive, or which would soil the mind of anyone who reads or hears it.

Help me never to pander to that which is low, never to seek popularity at the expense of truth, never to be more concerned with sensations than with facts, and always to respect the feelings and the rights of other people.

Grant that all that I write or say be such that it can stand the scrutiny of my own conscience, and such that I could with a clear conscience offer it to you.

This I ask for your love's sake. AMEN.

A PRAYER FOR ANIMALS

O God, you have made all living things, and you love them all.

Bless all living creatures, especially those in the service and in the homes of men.

Grant that no one may ever be thoughtlessly, callously, or deliberately cruel to the dumb animals who have no voice to speak and no power to defend themselves from the actions of humans.

Grant that those who keep animals as pets within their homes may care for them as they ought to be cared for, may never neglect them, or cause them needless suffering and pain.

Bless all animals in captivity, and grant that their masters and their trainers may always be kind.

The animals have given to us their strength and their work, and often even their devotion and their love; grant that we may give to them the care which they deserve as creatures whom your hands have made and for whom your heart cares.

This I ask for your love's sake. AMEN.

PRAYERS FOR
HELP AND HEALING

BEFORE GOING TO THE DOCTOR

O God,
I can no longer pretend to myself
  that everything will be all right
  if I just leave things alone.
I can no longer avoid the fact
  that there is something wrong.
Go with me when I go to my doctor today,
  and give me courage to face the truth about myself.
Make me quite sure that, whatever the verdict,
  I can face it with you.

Let me remember the promise of God:
  When you pass through the waters I will be with you.
                                        Isaiah 43:2

  My times are in thy hand:
  Why should I doubt or fear?
  My Father's hand will never cause
  His child a needless tear.

ON LEARNING THAT HOSPITAL
TREATMENT IS NECESSARY

O God, my Father,
Now that I know that I must go into hospital,
  help me not to worry.
Help me to realize
  that worry only makes things worse,
  and that the more I worry
  the longer I will take to get better.
Teach me that I am just as near you
  in a hospital bed as in my own home.
Give me that peace of mind
  without which I know that I can't have health of body.

Let me learn what Paul learned:
  I have learned, in whatever state I am, to be content.
                                        Philippians 4:11

  Give to the winds thy fears;
  Hope, and be undismayed;
  God hears thy sighs and counts thy tears,
  God shall lift up thy head.

AFTER ENTERING HOSPITAL

O God,
Everything is new and strange and rather frightening.
Half the time I don't know what is going on.
Help me
　to be serene and calm and relaxed.
Keep me cheerful,
　and help me to be a comrade
　to those who are feeling
　just as strange and just as afraid as I am.
Help me
　not to grumble or complain.
Help me
　not to be fussy and demanding.
Help me
　to be grateful for all that is done for me.
Help me
　to make the work of those who are looking after
　　me as easy as I can.
Help me
　to forget my own troubles
　　in doing something to help and cheer
　　those who are worse off than I am.

Help me to be as sure of God as the Psalmist was when he
　said:
　God is our refuge and strength,
　a very present help in trouble.

Psalm 46:1

　Hold thou my hands!
In grief and joy, in hope and fear,
Lord, let me feel that thou art near;
　Hold thou my hands!

BEFORE AN OPERATION

O God,
  Help me to remember at this moment
  that I have a very great deal to be thankful for.
I am grateful
  for the wisdom of the physician,
  and the skill of the surgeon,
  and the art of the anaesthetist,
  and the kindness of the nurses.
I am grateful for the merciful oblivion
  which anaesthetics bring.
Help me
  to be calm and relaxed,
  trusting the surgeon,
  and the skill you gave him,
  and trusting you.
And make me quite sure
  that, whatever happens,
Nothing can separate me
  from your love in Christ Jesus, my Lord.

Let me pray Jesus' own prayer:
  Father, into thy hands I commit my spirit!

Luke 23:46

  Tell me thou art mine, O Saviour,
  Grant me an assurance clear;
  Banish all my dark misgivings,
  Still my doubting, calm my fear.

AFTER AN OPERATION

O God,
Operations are all in the day's work
  for the surgeon and the doctor,
  and the anaesthetist and the nurse,
but for people like me
  they are strange and alarming.
I am so glad
  that I am through my operation,
  and that I am still alive!
I can say that to you,
  knowing that you will understand.
I know that this is only the first step
  on the way back to health.
Help me from now on.
  to be a good patient,
  thankful and uncomplaining,
  always helping, never hindering
  those who are trying to make me well.

Let me remember the confidence of the Psalmist:
  Why are you cast down, O my soul,
    and why are you disquieted within me?
  hope in God; for I shall praise him,
    my help and my God.

Psalm 43:5

God merciful and righteous is,
  yea, gracious is our Lord,
God saves the meek; I was brought low,
  he did me help afford.

FOR ONE IN A TIME OF
NERVOUS AND PHYSICAL EXHAUSTION

O God,
  my body won't act
  and my mind won't think,
  and I feel that I can't do anything.
  I'm too tired even to sleep.
The worst of it is that I feel
  that I will never be able to do anything again.
I get so utterly depressed.
  I've almost stopped hoping
  that I'll ever be fit again;
  and it doesn't seem worth while even trying.
Nothing seems to do any good,
  and there seems nothing left to do
  but to give up and to give in.
O God,
  Lighten my darkness;
  Strengthen my weakness;
  Put hope into my hopelessness.
  I'm beaten, unless you help me.
  Help me to believe that you will,
  Hear this my prayer through Jesus Christ our Lord.

Let me remember the experience of the Psalmist:
  I waited patiently for the Lord:
  He inclined to me and heard my cry.
  He put a new song in my mouth,
  A song of praise to our God.

Psalm 40:1, 3

The secret of living:
  To feel that though I journey on
  By stony paths and rugged ways,
  Thy blessed feet have gone before
  And strength is given for weary days.

IN NERVOUS TENSION

O God,
I just can't sleep.
I just can't stop thinking.
I just can't stop being afraid of the future.
I can't cope with things any longer,
   and I have got to a stage
   when I can't even rest.
I know that in the long run
   pills and drugs and sedatives
   are not really a cure.
Put your rest in my mind
   and your peace in my heart,
   that I may lean back
   and rest in you.

Let me take the advice of the Psalmist:
   Cast your burden on the Lord,
   and he will sustain you.

Psalm 55:22

   When in the night I sleepless lie,
   My soul with heavenly thoughts supply;
   Let no ill dreams disturb my rest,
   No powers of darkness me molest.

FOR ONE WITH A
NERVOUS BREAKDOWN

O God,
I've reached the stage
  when I just can't cope any longer,
  and it had to be this hospital for me.
I am so utterly tired
  and I can't concentrate.
My mind is so weary
  that I can't keep it on anything,
  and I can't control my thoughts.
The smallest task sets me worrying;
  things are always on the top of me.
The least thing irritates me,
  and I fly into a temper.
I get so depressed
  that I cry and can't stop crying.
I'm afraid of everything,
  afraid to meet people,
  afraid to go out,
  afraid to take a decision,
  afraid even to cross the street.
I just can't stop worrying.
I know that a mind is worse to cure than a body.
Help me to help myself
  by doing everything I can
  to cooperate with those who are trying to help me.
And, more than anything else,
  Give me the peace of mind
  which comes from thinking
  not of myself but of you.

I remember that Jesus said: Why are you afraid? Why have you
  no faith? Let me remember that he also said: Peace! Be still!
Mark 4:40, 39

'Tis only in thee hiding
I feel myself secure;
Only in thee abiding,
The conflict can endure.

Thine arm the victory gaineth
O'er every hateful foe;
Thy love my heart sustaineth
In all its cares and woe.

WHEN LIFE HAS
LOST ITS SWEETNESS

O God,
  Somehow things have gone all wrong.
I am always tired,
  and because I am tired
I am irritable,
  and because I am irritable
  there is always trouble between me
  and the people I live with.
I am always conscious of my body.
I have almost forgotten what it is like
  to feel fit and full of energy and life.
I have got to drive myself
  to do the work that used to be a pleasure.
I have got to toil at things
  that I used to do easily.
I used to be on top of my work,
  now it's on the top of me.
I used to enjoy life,
  but now life is a weariness.
O God,
  in hospital help me to find new strength
  and new zest for life.
Make me a good patient,
  so that I may help those
  who are doing their best to help me.

Let me remember that God's Spirit is on God's messenger to give
  to all sufferers a garland instead of ashes, the oil of gladness
  instead of mourning, the mantle of praise instead of a faint
  spirit.

Isaiah 61:3

Thy promise is my only plea,
With this I venture nigh;
Thou callest burdened souls to thee,
And such, O Lord, am I!

IN ANXIETY AND DEPRESSION

O God,
Sometimes I lie here and worry.
I worry
  about what is going to happen to myself,
  about what is going to happen to my work and to my job,
  and to those who are depending on me.
I worry
  about what is going to happen to the house and home,
  and about what is happening to the family
  with me not there.
After all, it would hardly be natural
  if I didn't.
I feel the worst,
  and sometimes I wonder
  if I am ever going to be well and strong again.
Give me
  the peace of mind
  which comes
  from leaving things to you.
Help me
  to feel the clasp of the everlasting arms
  underneath and about me.
  and to know
  that neither I nor those I love
  can ever drift
  beyond your love and care.

Let me remember the promise of Jesus:
  Peace I leave with you; my peace I give to you; not as the world
  gives do I give to you. Let not your hearts be troubled, neither
  let them be afraid.   *John 14:27*

  I know not what the future hath
  Of marvel or surprise,
  Assured alone that life and death
  His mercy underlies.

IN BITTERNESS AND RESENTMENT

O God,
It is better to speak frankly about things
   than to bottle them up.
I can't help wondering
   why this should have happened to me.
I can't help feeling bitter and resentful.
I know that I shouldn't feel that way,
And I don't really want to feel that way.
I can't help feeling angry
   when people who have never known any trouble
   come and tell me
   that it is all for the best.
Whatever happens, keep me
   from querulous self-pity.
At least teach me
   that I have got to accept things,
   whether I like it or not,
   and bring me in the end
   to that faith
   which can accept even what it cannot understand.

Let me remember Moses' song:
   The eternal God is your dwelling-place,
   and underneath are the everlasting arms.

Deuteronomy 33:27

When we in darkness walk,
Nor feel the heavenly flame,
Then is the time to trust our God
And rest upon his name.

IN PAIN AND
PHYSICAL DISTRESS

———————

Lord Jesus,
You know what pain is like.
You know
    the torture of the scourge upon your back,
    the sting of the thorns upon your brow,
    the agony of the nails in your hands.
You know what I'm going through just now.
Help me
    to bear my pain
    gallantly, cheerfully and patiently,
And help me to remember
    that I will never be tried
    above what I am able to bear,
    and that you are with me,
    even in this valley of the deep dark shadow.

Let me remember what Paul said:
    God is faithful, and he will not let you be
    tested beyond your strength.

1 Corinthians 10:13

    In ev'ry pang that rends the heart,
    The Man of Sorrows had a part;
    He sympathizes with our grief,
    And to the suff'rer sends relief.

WHEN SLEEP WILL NOT COME

O God,
   When you've got a worried mind
   and a body you can't forget,
      it's not easy to sleep,
   and the trouble is,
      the more you try to sleep.
      the less you can sleep.
Thank you
   for those who watch all night
   to care for me,
      and for people like me.
Thank you
   for books to read
      when I can't sleep.
O God,
   stop my thoughts
      going round and round;
   stop my body
      being all tensed and strained.
If I must think,
   help me to think of your love,
   and of Jesus here with me all the time,
      so that, even if I can't sleep,
      I will be at peace.

Let me think about what the Psalmist said:
   Even the darkness is not dark to thee,
      the night is bright as the day;
      for darkness is as light with thee.

Psalm 139:12

Thee, in the watches of the night,
When I remember on my bed,
Thy presence makes the darkness light;
Thy guardian wings are round my head.

IN HOMESICKNESS

O God,
I can't help lying here
  and thinking about home.
I can't relax here
  the way I can relax at home,
    because everything is so strange.
I keep wondering
  how they are getting on without me,
and if they are worrying about me
  as much as I am worrying about them.
I wouldn't be human
  if I didn't miss my own home
    and my own people.
But help me to be sensible and to realize
  that the more I worry,
    and the more discontented I am,
      the slower will be my cure,
        and the longer I will be getting back to them.
And help me to remember
  that there are other people in this ward
    who are homesick too.
So help me to forget my own loneliness
  in doing something which will help them
    to forget theirs.

Let me remember and let me echo Paul's great claim:
  I have learned, in whatever state I am, to be content.
                                        Philippians 4:11

  My times are in thy hand;
  My God I wish them there;
  My life, my friends, my soul I leave
  Entirely to thy care.

FOR HOME AND FAMILY

O God,
I think that just about the worst thing about this
  is being separated from my family and my home.
Keep my husband/wife from worrying too much about me,
And keep the children from missing me too much.
Help me to realize
  that things will go on,
  even if I am not there,
And that it is not for all that long anyway.
Thank you
  for giving me good neighbours, good friends, good
    relations,
  to look after things and to help,
  when I am not there.
Help me to remember
  that the more I worry about them,
    the slower will be my recovery
      and the longer I will take to get back to them,
And help me
  to lie back and to relax
  for as long as I need,
  in the certainty that
  although I am separated from them
  you are still with them and me.

Let me remember the word of Jesus:
  They shall never perish, and no one shall
  snatch them out of my hand.

John 10:28

  Guard them from every harm
  When dangers shall assail,
  And teach them that thy power
  Can never, never fail;
  We cannot with our loved ones be,
  But trust them, Father, unto thee.

FOR ONE WITH NO ONE
AT HOME TO CARE

O God,
I have no one of my own at all now,
There isn't anyone to think about me
 or to worry about me.
I have friends and acquaintances,
 but I have no one at home
 of my own flesh and blood.
I'm not worried about being looked after.
I know that that will be done all right.
 But I can't help feeling lonely,
 and I can't help envying others
 who have people who really care for them.
Help me to remember that
 I have you as my Father,
And that I have Jesus
 as the Brother born to help
 in time of trouble.
And so help me to lose my loneliness
 in your love.

I can say with the Psalmist:
 Whom have I in heaven but thee?
 And there is nothing upon earth that
 I desire beside thee.

Psalm 73:25

 I've found a friend; O such a friend!
 He loved me ere I knew him;
He drew me with the cords of love,
 And thus he bound me to him;
And round my heart still closely twine
 These ties which nought can sever,
For I am his, and he is mine,
 For ever and for ever.

FOR ONE WHO HAS RETURNED HOME

O God,
From this illness of mine I have learned one thing anyway –
   that you have got to lose a thing for a time
   in order to value it when you get it back
I never really appreciated my home until now.
   It's lovely to be back home;
   it's lovely to see and touch
     the old familiar things,
   and to be again with the people I love.
Help me to avoid two things.
Help me to avoid
   trying to do too much
     in order to show how well I am,
   and so undoing all the good
     that has been done to me in hospital.
And help me to avoid
   acting the invalid,
     and expecting to be waited on hand and foot.
Give me a grateful heart
and a sensible mind,
   and help me to make steady progress,
     until I am a hundred per cent fit again.

Like the Psalmist I am glad because
   God setteth the solitary in families.

Psalm 68:6

Help us, O Lord, our homes to make
Thy Holy Spirit's dwelling-place;
Our hands and hearts devotion take
To be the servants of thy grace.
Teach us to keep our homes so fair,
That were our Lord a child once more,
He might be glad our hearth to share,
And find a welcome at our door.

WHEN HUMAN HELP IS VAIN
AND GOD ALONE REMAINS

O God,
I think that everyone has done all that can be done,
  and I have the feeling
  that it is not enough.
So I'm coming to you now
  because I have nowhere else to go.
Make me quite sure that, whatever happens,
nothing can separate me from you,
that, whether I get better or not,
I am in your hands.
Help me
  not to be afraid any more,
  and not to worry any more.
I'm not giving in:
I'll still hold on to life,
  and do everything to get well.
But make me sure that,
  whether I live or die,
you are with me always,
  to the end – and beyond the end.

Let me remember the faith of the Psalmist:
  In peace I will both lie down and sleep,
  for thou alone, O Lord, makest me dwell in safety.

Psalm 4:8

  Abide with me: fast falls the eventide;
  The darkness deepens; Lord with me abide:
  When other helpers fail, and comforts flee,
  Help of the helpless, O abide with me.

A PRAYER FOR ONE
WHO IS BLIND

O God, I have to live in the dark now, and there is much that I can't help missing.

I can't help missing the faces of my loved ones and my friends, and the colour of the flowers. I can't help feeling it difficult not to see the road that I must walk and the scenes I loved.

O God, help me to face all this with courage and with cheerfulness.

I thank you for all that is done for us blind people. I thank you for books in Braille, for guide dogs wonderfully trained to be wise, for special training to make us able to do a useful job, for the sympathy and the kindness and the consideration which nearly everyone shows to us.

I thank you that my memory has still its gallery of pictures and that the eyes of my mind can still see. Even if I can no longer see the things that are visible, I can still see the things that are invisible.

Keep me from pitying myself, and help me not to let this thing beat me. Help me bravely to train myself to be as independent as it is possible for me to be. I know that no trial ever came to any man without bringing with it the power to bear it. Help me to bear and to conquer this.

This I ask for the sake of him who is the light of the world, for Jesus' sake.   AMEN.

A PRAYER FOR ONE
WHO IS DEAF

O God, life has taken away from me the power to hear, and there is much that I have lost.

I miss the voices of my friends, the music that I loved, the many lovely and homely sounds which others hear.

Sometimes my deafness makes me avoid company, and sometimes it makes things very awkward for me. Sometimes I think that deaf people get less sympathy than anyone else, and that people regard us deaf people as something of a nuisance. It is very easy for a deaf person like me to become lonely and suspicious and to avoid meeting people.

O God, help me to bear it all with a good grace. After all I have got something to be thankful for. I can sleep anywhere, because noise doesn't disturb me, and I can concentrate on my work because sounds don't distract me. When I think about it, I have got some blessings to count!

Help me to do my best to conquer this handicap. Help me at least to be sensible enough to do what I can about it. I thank you very specially for hearing aids, and for the skill of those who have done so much to help us deaf people to hear.

Help me to do my work and to enjoy my life, even although I cannot hear without my hearing aid.

This I ask for Jesus' sake. AMEN.

FOR ONE WHO IS
CRITICALLY ILL

O God,
They don't need to tell me
   that it is going to be touch and go with me.
I know quite well
   that I've got to be ready for anything.
I know that the surgeons and the doctors and the nurses
   will do their very best for me.
Give me the will to win through.
Give me
   patience to bear my weakness,
   courage to endure my pain,
   obedience to accept whatever is best for me.
If I am not to get better,
   make me quite sure that,
   whether I live or die,
   nothing can separate me from your love.
I think that I have got past the stage of worrying,
But I know how anxious those who love me are,
Bless them and help them not to worry,
   but to leave everything to you;
   because that is what I am doing.

Let me remember the word of the prophet:
   Thou dost keep him in perfect peace;
   whose mind is stayed on thee,
   because he trusts in thee.

Isaiah 26:3

I am trusting thee, Lord Jesus;
Never let me fall;
I am trusting thee for ever,
and for all.

WHEN HEALING IS SLOW
AND LONG DELAYED

O God,
I know that recovery cannot be quick.
I know that the body
takes its own time to heal.
But I know
  that everything possible is being done for me.
All the same
  I get impatient.
I want
  to be on my feet;
I want
  to be home again;
I want
  to get back to my work.
O God,
  teach me what I know already.
Teach me
  that the more impatient I am,
  the more I delay my recovery.
Help me to learn to wait
  cheerfully and hopefully and uncomplainingly,
    content to live one day
    and to take one step at a time.

Let me remember the Psalmist:
  Wait for the Lord;
  be strong, and let your heart take courage;
  yea, wait for the Lord!

Psalm 27:14

  Trust in the Lord, for ever trust,
    and banish all your fears;
  Strength in the Lord Jehovah dwells
    eternal as his years.

FOR ONE TO WHOM STRENGTH
IS SLOW IN COMING BACK

O God,
I'm all right
so long as I am lying here in bed,
or so long as I don't try to do anything;
    but I have just no strength.
I can't hurry;
    I can't even do anything quickly;
    I have always to take my time –
        and it is a long time.
It is so discouraging
    always to feel weak,
    and always to feel tired.
I want to get back to work,
    there is so much that I want to do,
    and so much that is waiting to be done.
O God,
give me the patience
that I know I must have.
Make me a little better every day,
and able to do a little more each day,
    until, bit by bit,
    I can shoulder the tasks of life again.

The prophet said:
    They who wait for the Lord shall renew their strength.

Isaiah 40:31

O God, make this true for me.

    Art thou weary, art thou languid,
        Art thou sore distressed?
    'Come to me' saith One, 'and coming,
        Be at rest.'

FOR ONE WHO KNOWS
THAT HE IS A DIFFICULT PATIENT

O God,
When I think about myself,
 I am ashamed of myself.
Because I am so nervous and afraid,
 I am more demanding
  than I have any right to be.
Because I have become selfish,
 because all my life people have been too good to me,
  I think that no one matters but me.
Because I am far too self-willed,
 I don't cooperate as I ought
  with those who are doing their best for me.
Sometimes – often – I can be
 impatient, complaining, discontented,
 ungrateful, disobedient.
O God,
I can see all this,
 when I lie thinking about myself.
But somehow I do the things
 I don't want to do,
and I behave in a way that I know is wrong
 even when I am doing it.
Help me to conquer myself.
Give me
 patience, serenity, unselfishness,
 obedience, contentment, gratitude
  for all that is done for me.
Help me
 from now on not to be difficult,
 but to try to make things easier
  for those who are doing so much for me.

Let me take to myself the advice to Timothy:
 Aim at righteousness, godliness, faith, love, steadfastness,
 gentleness.
                                          I Timothy 6:11

Hidden in the hollow
  Of his blessed hand,
Never foe can follow,
  Never traitor stand;

Not a surge of worry,
  Not a shade of care,
Not a blast of hurry,
  Touch the spirit there.

A PRAYER FOR ONE
WHO IS HELPLESS OR BED-RIDDEN

O God, life has taken a good deal from me, but I want to begin by thanking you for all that life has left me.

I can see and read; I can hear and listen; I can talk and speak with my friends. Though my body must stay in the one place, I can still send my mind and my imagination in adventurous travel. Once I was too busy doing things to think. Now I can think until I reach you and the things which really matter.

I have still books which I can read, music I can listen to, wireless and television which I can hear and watch, even games which I can play in bed.

For all that, O God, I need your help more than I need anything else. Keep me cheerful even when it is very difficult. Keep me content when my whole being naturally wants to be resentful. Let me not become querulous, complaining, demanding. Keep me from self-pity. Help me to be truly grateful for all that is done for me; and, even when it is the last thing that I feel like doing, help me to smile.

Bless the doctors and the nurses and the people who care for me and who look after me; and give them skill to find a cure some day even for people like me.

When I feel that I am useless and a burden to others, help me to remember that I can still pray, and so help me constantly to uphold the hands of those I love, and constantly to bear them and myself to your throne of grace.

All this I ask for your love's sake. AMEN.

WHEN HELPLESS AND BEDRIDDEN

O God,
Even when I am lying here like this in bed,
   help me to count my blessings.
I can still talk,
   and use my hands quite a bit.
I can still send my mind and my imagination
   where my body can't go.
I can still remember,
   and I can still pray.
Help me
   not to grumble,
   not to complain,
   not to whine.
Keep me cheerful,
   and help me to make things as easy as I can
   for the people who have to look after me,
   and the people who come to see me.
And when things get so bad
   that I do want to break down and to break out,
help me to do it
   when there is no one there to see it but you,
   because I know you will understand.
Even on this bed
   give me the joy
      that nothing and no one can take from me.

Help me to remember and to believe what Jesus promised: So you
   have sorrow now, but I will see you again, and your hearts will
   rejoice, and no one will take your joy from you.

John 16:22

Nor death, nor life, nor earth, nor hell,
   nor time's destroying sway,
Shall e'er efface us from his heart,
   or make his love decay.

FOR ONE WHO IS
PUZZLED AND PERPLEXED

O God,
Sometimes I can't help wondering
why this should have happened to me.
You get a lot of time to think
  when you are lying in a hospital bed,
and you see a lot of things
  in a hospital.
And sometimes I can't help wondering
  why there is so much suffering and pain
    in the world.
I know that there just isn't any answer to these questions, at
    least just now.
So help me to accept
  what I can't understand.
And help me to be sure
  that this is not the only world,
and that there is some place
  where the broken things are mended,
  where the lost things are found,
  where all the questions are answered,
  where all the problems are solved,
  where we know, even as we are known.
So in this world help me
  to leave it all to you,
in the certainty that I will never be tried
  beyond what you will make me able to bear.

Give me the Psalmist's certainty:
  Even though I walk through the valley of the shadow of death,
  I will fear no evil: for thou art with me; thy rod and thy staff,
  they comfort me.

Psalm 23:4

In heavenly love abiding,
  No change my heart shall fear;
And safe is such confiding,
  For nothing changes here:

The storm may roar without me,
  My heart may low be laid;
But God is round about me,
  And can I be dismayed?

FOR COURAGE

Give me, O God,
   All the courage I need in this place.
Give me courage
   To bear discomfort without grumbling,
     and pain without complaint.
Give me courage
   To bear uncertainty with hope,
     and long delays with patience.
Give me courage
   To keep on trusting when I cannot understand,
And help me always to remember
   that, in this as in everything,
   it is the one who sticks it out gallantly to the end
   who will be saved.

Let me remember the word of Jesus:
   He who endures to the end will be saved.

Matthew 24:13

   Sun of our life, thy quickening ray
   Sheds on our path the glow of day;
   Star of our hope, thy softened light
   Cheers the long watches of the night.

FOR COURAGE TO MEET
GROWING WEAKNESS

O God,
   I'm beginning to feel
     that I'm losing the battle.
My strength just won't come back,
and this body of mine is tired.
I know
   that they are doing their best for me.
I know
   that those who love me
     are thinking of me
     and praying for me
     all the time.
If it be possible,
   help me to pass the breaking-point
   and not to break,
   but, sunshine or shadow,
     I leave it to you.

Let me remember the confidence of the Psalmist:
   Even though I walk through the valley of deep darkness,
   I fear no evil, for thou art with me.

Psalm 23:4

   Thine arm, O Christ, in days of old
     Was strong to help and save;
   It triumphed o'er disease and death,
     O'er darkness and the grave.
   Be thou our great deliverer still,
     Thou Lord of life and death;
   Restore and quicken, soothe and bless,
     With thine almighty breath.

FOR FAITH

O God,
Sometimes I can't help feeling
  that I am one of these people Jesus meant
  when he talked about
  those who had little faith.
I am afraid of what might happen,
  and I haven't the faith that can face the future
  without a tremor.
Doubts get into my mind and heart,
  and I sometimes wonder
  if you do really care for me.
I suppose that, when illness like this comes,
  far more people than I wonder
  why this should have happened to them.
Sometimes I wonder if you can possibly hear my prayers.
There are so many people praying to you all at the one time.
And yet I know that
  I wouldn't be alive at all, and
  I couldn't have faced life at all
  by myself.
  And after all I wouldn't be talking to you now
  unless I had some faith.
Give me the perfect and serene confidence
  which can lean back and say:
  Into your hands I commit my spirit,
  for life and for death and for life to come.

Help me to remember the prayer that at least I can pray:
  I believe: help my unbelief!

Mark 9:24

  Other refuge have I none;
    Hangs my helpless soul on thee;
  Leave, ah! leave me not alone;
    Still support and comfort me.

FOR ACCEPTANCE
OF GOD'S WILL

————

O God,
Help me to say:
  Your will be done.
Help me
  to be quite sure
    that all things do work together for good.
Help me to remember and to discover
  that even pain and weakness
    can bring me nearer you,
  and that the dews of sorrow
    can be lustred by your love.
Help me to remember
  that it is your promise,
    that neither I nor anyone else
  will be tested above what we can bear.
Help me to remember
  that a father's hand will never cause
    his child a needless tear.
Help me
  to say, as my Blessed Lord said,
    Into your hands I commit my spirit.

Let me remember Jesus' last prayer:
  Father, into your hands I commit my spirit.

Luke 23:46

Not mine, not mine the choice,
  In things or great or small;
Be thou my guide and strength,
  My wisdom and my all.

FOR HOPE

O God,
It is very difficult to keep on hoping,
  when nothing seems to be happening.
And it is even more difficult
  when there seem to be more setbacks than progress.
Help me to have the hope
  that nothing can put out.
After all, even on the darkest night,
  no one ever doubts that the morning will come again;
and in the hardest winter
  no one ever doubts that spring is never far behind.
Help me to think
  of the skill you have given
    to those whose task it is to heal,
and of the essential toughness
  of this human body of mine.
Help me to remember
  that for you and with you
    nothing is impossible.
And help me to remember always
  that I have a hope
    that does not stop with this world,
      but goes on for ever.

Let me remember the Psalmist's confidence:
  Why are you cast down, O my soul,
  and why are you disquieted within me?
  Hope in God; for I shall again praise him,
  my help and my God.   *Psalm 43:5*

  If thou but suffer God to guide thee,
    And hope in him through all thy ways,
  He'll give thee strength, whate'er betide thee,
    And bear thee through the evil days;
  Who trusts in God's unchanging love
  Builds on the rock that nought can move.

FOR ONE WHO IS GETTING BETTER

O God,
I want to thank you
   for bringing me this far along the road to recovery.
It is good to be able
   to get my feet on the floor again;
It is good to be able
   to do at least some things for myself again.
It is best of all
   just to have the joy of feeling well again.
O God,
keep me grateful,
  grateful to all the people
  who helped me back to health;
grateful to you
  for the way in which
  you have brought me through it all.
O God,
still give me patience.
Help me
  not to be in too big a hurry to do too much.
Help me
  to keep on doing what I'm told to do.
Help me
  to be so obedient to those who know
  what is best for me, that very soon
  I shall be on the top of the world
  and on the top of my job again.

I can say what the Psalmist said:
  I waited patiently for the Lord;
  he inclined to me and heard my cry.　　　　*Psalm 40:1*

He took me from a fearful pit,
  and from the miry clay,
And on a rock he set my feet,
  establishing my way.

FOR ONE WHO HAS REALIZED
THAT HE IS GROWING OLD

O God,
It seems like yesterday
   that I went out to work for the first time;
and now I haven't much longer to go,
   and I'm well over the halfway line.
I can't shut my eyes to the fact
   that I'm getting older.
Physically, I get more easily tired,
   and any effort becomes more and more of an effort.
Mentally, I'm slower;
   I can't work for so long at a time;
     and concentration is more difficult.
First and foremost, help me to realize quite clearly
   what I can do and what I can't do,
   and to accept my necessary limitations.
And then help me to be thankful
   for all that the years have given me,
     and for all the experience that life has brought me.
Help me to use what is left to me of life
   wisely and well;
for time is short now,
   and I dare not waste any of it.

Let me remember what the prophet said:
   Your old men shall dream dreams,
   And your young men shall see visions.

Joel 2:28

Long as my life shall last,
   Teach me thy way!
Where'er my lot be cast,
   Teach me thy way!
Until the race is run,
Until the journey's done,
Until the crown is won,
   Teach me thy way!

WHEN GROWING OLD

O God,
I know now what it is like
to be growing old.
Everything is a bigger effort
than it used to be.
I get more easily tired,
and each job takes longer to do.
My memory is not so good;
My mind is not so quick;
My body is not so strong.
And yet I've got a lot to be thankful for.
I have learned
what is important
and what is not important.
I know now
that there are a great many things
not worth worrying about.
I have learned
to take the rough with the smooth
and not to get upset.
I have learned
who my real friends are,
and how much I owe to those who love me,
and to those whom I love.
Above all, when I look back
I can see your hand in everything,
and when I remember all that you have done for me in the past
it's easy to trust you
for the days to come.

Isaiah heard God saying:
Even to your old age I am He,
and to grey hairs I will carry you,
I have made and I will bear
I will carry and save.

Isaiah 46:4

Under the shadow of thy throne,
  Thy saints have dwelt secure;
Sufficient is thine arm alone,
  And our defence is sure.

FOR ONE WHO IS
OLD AND DEPENDENT

O God,
I have come to the stage
  when I can no longer work,
    and when I can no longer even look after myself.
    I am not ill;
    I am just old.
  My body has no strength in it;
  my memory has grown forgetful;
  and sometimes my mind won't think.
Sometimes I feel very lonely,
  because there are so few
  of my friends and loved ones left.
And yet I have a lot to be thankful for.
  I have had a long day, and a good day's work.
  I am grateful that there are places like this,
  and I am grateful for the care of doctors and nurses
    who have devoted themselves
    to the care of those who are old;
  and I am grateful for the visits of people
    who have not forgotten me.
You have left me still here.
  Help me to accept life as it is;
and help me to live in the evening time of life
  with cheerfulness and with serenity,
    and without complaint,
    until the day closes
      and you take me home to you.

Let the prayer of the Psalmist be my prayer:
  So even to old age and grey hairs,
  O God, do not forsake me.

Psalm 71:18

With mercy and with judgement
  My web of time he wove,
And aye the dews of sorrow
  Were lustred by his love;

I'll bless the hand that guided,
  I'll bless the heart that planned,
When throned where glory dwelleth
  In Immanuel's land.

FOR THE POWER
TO SUFFER AND TO TRIUMPH

O God,
I don't want anything startling or heroic;
I just want to be able to bear things.
They can do a lot for me,
but sometimes even their drugs don't work.
Help me to bear things
  without grumbling;
  without complaining;
  without whining;
  without self-pity, like a good soldier.
Help me
  to pass the breaking-point and not to break.
You know all about it, Lord Jesus.
You knew
  the mental agony of Gethsemane.
You knew
  the physical pain of the lash,
  of the crown of thorns, of the nails.
I know that you won't mind me saying
  that I'm glad you went through it all,
  because it means that you can understand exactly how I feel.
I know that in the end
  all things pass;
Till then, make me brave.
I wait for your promise of the time
  when there will be no more pain.

The Psalmist said:
  I kept my faith, even when I said, I am greatly afflicted.
  Help me too to keep my faith.   *Psalm 116:10*

  No pain that we can share
  But he has felt its smart,
  All forms of human grief and care
  Have pierced that tender heart.

FOR ONE ANXIOUS
ABOUT BUSINESS OR EMPLOYMENT

O God,
I think that the trouble about lying here like this
is that I am more worried about other people
    than I am about myself.
I can't help thinking what is going to happen
    to my wife and children,
    with so much less money coming in.
I can't help wondering what will happen
    if I come out of here
    not able for my old job.
I can't help wondering what will happen
    to those who depend on me
    if I don't come out at all.
It's all very well to talk
    about peace and not worrying,
But I wouldn't be human
    if I didn't feel like this –
    and I'm quite sure you understand.
But help me all the same to remember
    that, if I worry,
I am only making things worse,
    and spoiling my own chances.
So help me
    to take it one day at a time,
    and to leave the unknown future to you.

Let me remember the words of Jesus:
    Do not be anxious about tomorrow, for tomorrow will be
    anxious for itself. Let the day's own troubles be sufficient
    for the day.
                          Matthew 6:34

FOR ONE
WHO IS GOING BLIND

O God,
It is hard to think of a world
   in which I cannot see the sun and the flowers,
   and the faces of those I love
It is hard to think of a life
   in which I cannot read or watch things,
   or see lovely things any more.
But even in the dark there will be something left.
I can still have memory,
   and I can still see things again
   with my mind's eye.
I thank you for all that skill and kindness
   do for people like me.
I thank you for Braille, which keeps the world of books
   from being altogether closed to me.
I thank you that I will still be able
   to hear the voices that I know
   and to touch the things and the people I love.
Lord Jesus you are the Light of Life;
   Be with me in the dark.

Let me remember what Jesus said:
   I am the light of the world; he who follows me will not
   walk in darkness, but will have the light of life.

John 8:12

   Light of the world! for ever, ever shining,
      There is no change in thee;
   True Light of Life, all joy and health enshrining
      Thou canst not fade nor flee.

FOR ONE WHO HAS
LOST THE POWER TO SPEAK

———

O God,
I cannot speak to you in words,
but I can still send my thoughts to you;
  and, although I can't say the words out loud,
  I know that you will hear.
Life can be very difficult
  when you can't speak.
Not to be able to tell people what I want;
Not to be able to ask or answer a question;
Not to be able to talk to friends and dear ones;
  To have the barrier of silence on my lips –
    It is very difficult.
Thank you, O God, for what is left –
  for writing;
  for the language of signs;
    for those who have learned to read my lips.
Help me to bear this that has happened to me,
and to accept it and not to feel frustrated.
Thank you
  for the people who are kind to me;
Thank you
  for making me sure
  that you can hear the words
    that I can't speak,
    and the things I can think
      but can not say.

Let me remember that words are unnecessary with God, for,
  as the Psalmist said to God:
Thou discernest my thoughts from afar.

Psalm 139:2

Prayer is the burden of a sigh,
  The falling of a tear,
The upward glancing of an eye
  When none but God is near.

FOR ONE WHO IS GOING DEAF

O God,
The trouble about being deaf is that most people
find deaf people just a nuisance.
 They sympathize with people
 who are blind and lame;
 but they just get irritated and annoyed
 with people who are deaf.
And the result of this is
 that deaf people are apt to avoid company,
 and so get more and more lonely,
 and more and more shut in.
Help me now that my hearing has begun to go.
Help me
 to face the situation
 and to realize that there is no good trying to hide it,
 for that will only make it worse and worse.
Help me
 to be grateful for all that can be done
 for deaf people like me.
If I have got to wear a hearing aid,
 Help me to do it quite naturally,
 and not be shy or embarrassed about it.
Give me the perseverance
 not to let this trouble get me down,
 and not to let it cut me off from others.
And help me to remember
 that, whatever happens,
 there is nothing can stop me hearing your voice.

Even if I cannot hear the voices of men, let me remember
 Samuel and say: Speak, for thy servant hears. *I Samuel 3:10*

 Hear him ye deaf; his praise, ye dumb,
  Your loosened tongues employ;
 Ye blind, behold your Saviour come;
  And leap, ye lame, for joy!

FOR ONE WHO IS CRIPPLED

O God,
Sometimes I can't help thinking
  about the things I miss,
because I am tied to this house,
  and can't move around now.
I miss the open air and the open road,
  and the feel of the sun and the wind and the rain.
I miss going to work and going to the shops.
I miss playing and watching games.
I miss the church on Sunday.
Still, I know that I have a lot of things left.
My body may be tied to the one place,
  but I can still send my mind and my thoughts
    and my imagination
    adventuring anywhere.
I've got books to read,
  wireless to listen to, television to watch,
I've got good friends
  who never forget to come to see me.
Help me to remember that,
  even if I can't be anything else,
I can at least be cheerful.
Help me not to be too sorry for myself,
  and always to keep smiling.

Let me remember the Psalmist:
  The Lord lifts up those who are bowed down.

Psalm 146:8

Rest of the weary, joy of the sad;
Hope of the dreary, light of the glad;
Home of the stranger, strength to the end;
Refuge from danger, Saviour and friend.

FOR ONE INJURED
IN AN ACCIDENT

O God,
I never thought when I went out that morning
that I would finish up here in this hospital.
Now I really know
   that life is an uncertain business,
and that you never know
   what is going to happen.
I don't really know whether the whole thing was my fault,
   or whether someone else was to blame.
Don't let me start wondering about that.
Just let me accept this,
   and do everything I can
   to help my own progress.
Help those who love me
   to get over the shock
   that this must have been to them.
Help them not to worry,
   but to be sure
   that I'm in good hands here.
And when I get out of here
   help me to remember to be a lot more careful,
   so that I won't get involved in an accident
   and so that I won't be the cause of an accident
   to anyone else.
I am very grateful that I am still alive,
   and that things are no worse than they are.
Help me to be a good patient
   so that I will soon be on my feet again.

The Sage was right when he said:
   You do not know what a day may bring forth.

Proverbs 27:1

But in spite of that, help me to say:
   Peace, perfect peace, our future all unknown?
   Jesus, we know, and he is on the throne.

FOR THE ONE WHO IS LEFT

O God,
The trouble about life just now
  is that I seem to have all the things
  which don't matter,
    and I seem to have lost all the things
    which do matter.
I have life;
  I have money enough to live on;
    I have a job to do;
but I am alone,
  and sometimes I feel that nothing
  can make up for that.
O God,
compel me to see the meaning of my faith.
  Make me realize that
    I have a hope as well as a memory;
  that the unseen cloud of witnesses is around me;
    that Jesus meant it when he said
    that he would always be with me.
And make me realize that
  so long as you leave me here
there is something that I am meant to do;
  and in doing it, help me to find
    the comfort and the courage
    that I need to go on.

Let me remember Paul's confidence:
  But we would not leave you ignorant, brethren, concerning
  those who are asleep, that you may not grieve as others do
  who have no hope. For since we believe that Jesus died
  and rose again, even so, through Jesus, God will bring with
  him those who have fallen asleep.
                                I Thessalonians 4:13, 14

'Midst pastures green he'll lead his flock,
  Where living streams appear,
And God the Lord from every eye
  Shall wipe off every tear.

A PRAYER FOR THOSE
WHO HAVE THEIR HEALTH

O God,
Help me to be grateful
  for the things which come so regularly
  that we can forget that they are gifts.
Help me to be grateful
  for the things which so often we do not value
    until we lose them.
Above all, make me grateful to you for my health,
  for strength of body and for health of mind,
  for accuracy of hand and eye,
    and mind and brain,
      to do my work.
Give me sympathy for those who are ill;
and help me never to be impatient and annoyed
  and irritated
    with those who are not so strong as I am.
Help me to give my strength to the weak,
and grant that my own good health
  may never make me forget,
    those who are less fortunate than I am.

Job said:
  I was eyes to the blind,
  and feet to the lame,
  I was a father to the poor.
May that be my aim too.

Job 29:15, 16

  My health and friends and parents dear
    To me by God are given;
  I have not any blessing here
    But what is sent from heaven.

A PRAYER FOR ONE WHO
HAS A DIFFICULT PATIENT
TO NURSE

O God,
I needn't tell you how difficult . . . is.
He is irritable and impatient and demanding;
   whatever I do is wrong.
      He wouldn't be happy
      unless *he* had something to complain about.
   He will never even admit
      that *he* is making progress
      and feeling better.
O God,
give me patience,
   never to let myself be angered and upset;
give me sympathy,
   always to try to understand;
give me wisdom of mind,
   to help *him* through *his* difficult time.
Keep me from becoming annoyed,
   no matter what the provocation;
and help me always to keep on caring,
   even when there seems to be no response.
Hasten *his* cure
   in body and in mind,
so that the day will soon come
when the difficult time will be forgotten.
And, Lord Jesus, help me always to remember,
   that, whatever I have to bear,
it is nothing to the ingratitude and the thanklessness
   that you had to bear.

Let me think of what Peter said to those who had to work for
   others:
   Servants, be submissive to your masters with all respect, not
   only to the kind and gentle but also to the overbearing . . . For
   what credit is it, if when you do wrong and are beaten for it

you take it patiently? But if when you do right and suffer for it you take it patiently, you have God's approval.

I Peter 2:18–20

Though long the weary road we tread,
  And sorrow crown each lingering year,
No path we shun, no darkness dread,
  Our hearts still whispering, 'Thou art near.'

FOR ONE WHO KNOWS THAT HE WILL NEVER BE FULLY WELL AGAIN

O God,
I know that when I get back home
life is never going to be quite the same again.
I know
   that I will always have to take care;
   and that I will have to go much slower;
   and that I will not be able to make the efforts
     that I used to make.
Help me to be glad that I am as I am,
   and that I have got what I have.
I am still alive, and I can still work;
I can still move about;
I can still meet my friends,
   and see the beauty of the world.
I can see now
   that I was living at far too fast a pace,
   and at far too great a pressure.
So help me from now on
   to accept life as it is,
   and to make the best of it.
And help me to be sure that,
   if I go about it in the right way,
   life is not finished,
   but that the best is yet to be.

Let me remember what Paul said:
   I have learned, in whatever state I am, to be content.
Philippians 4:11

   I am content with what I have,
     Little be it or much;
   And, Lord, contentment still I crave,
     Because thou savest such.

A PRAYER FOR OTHER PATIENTS

O God,
Keep me from praying to you,
as if there was no one in this ward except me.
Help me to remember
    that I am only one person and one voice
    in this ward and in this hospital,
       and in a world in which
       there are so many people in trouble.
Bless everyone in this ward,
   Anyone who is lonely or frightened,
     anyone who is shy and nervous;
   anyone who is suffering a lot of pain;
     anyone who is making slow progress
       and who is discouraged;
   anyone who has had a setback today
    and who is disappointed;
   anyone who is worried and anxious;
     anyone for whom there is no recovery.
And help me to help others,
   and so to forget my own troubles,
   by sharing the troubles of others.

Let me remember Paul's advice:
   Bear one another's burdens, and so fulfil the law of Christ.
                                       Galatians 6:2

  In sickness, sorrow, want or care,
  Whate'er it be, 'tis ours to share;
  May we, where help is needed, there
    Give help as unto thee.

WHEN AWAITING A CHILD

O God,
The months of waiting are ended,
  and my time is almost here.
Take away all tension and fear,
  and make me relaxed and unafraid.
Strengthen me for my ordeal,
  and give me joy in remembering
  that through me you are sending
    another life into this world.

I remember that Jesus said:
  When a woman is in travail she has sorrow, because her hour
  has come; but when she is delivered of the child, she no longer
  remembers the anguish, for joy that a child is born into the
  world.

John 16:21

O Father, Thou who has created all
  In wisest love, we pray,
Look on this babe, who at Thy gracious call
  Is entered on life's way;
Bend o'er him in Thy tenderness,
Thine image on his soul impress;
O Father, hear.

WHEN A CHILD IS BORN

O God,
Thank you
   for bringing me and my baby
     safely through everything.
Bless my baby.
   Keep him/her safe
     in all the dangers of childhood.
   Bring him/her in safety to manhood/womanhood;
     and grant that some day
       he/she may do a good day's work in the world;
   and help me always to help him/her to see
     that Jesus is his/her friend.
Bless me.
   You have given me this great privilege;
   help me now to be true to my great responsibility,
     and never to fail in the trust you have given to me.
Help me, when I get home again,
   to make my home a place
   where Jesus is an unseen
     but an always remembered guest.

I remember today how Jesus said:
   Whoever receives one such child in my name receives me.
                     Matthew 18:5

   Grant us, then, pure hearts and patient,
     That, in all we do or say,
   Little souls our deeds may copy,
     And be never led astray;
   Little feet our steps may follow
     In a safe and narrow way.

A THANKSGIVING FOR JESUS,
THE RESURRECTION AND THE LIFE

Lord Jesus
  It is my great comfort to know
    that, where I have been,
    you have been before.
You had a day's work to do
  just as I have a day's work to do.
You were tempted
  just as I am tempted.
You were distressed in mind in Gethsemane
  just as I am distressed in mind.
You had to suffer pain
  just as I have to suffer pain
  and your pain was far worse than mine.
You are the Resurrection and the Life,
  because you died and rose again,
  and you are alive always and for ever,
    and once and for all you conquered death.
So I am quite sure that, whatever happens to me,
  you have been there;
  you are there;
  you will be there,
    to the end of time and beyond.

Jesus said to Martha:
  I am the Resurrection and the Life; he who believes in me,
  though he die, yet shall he live, and whoever lives and believes
  in me shall never die.

John 11:25, 26

  Thou art the Way, the Truth, the Life:
    Grant us that way to know
  That truth to keep, that life to win,
    Whose joys eternal flow.

A THANKSGIVING FOR JESUS
THE GOOD PHYSICIAN AND FOR ALL
WHO FOLLOW IN HIS STEPS

O God,
I thank you for Jesus, the Good Physician.
  I thank you that he restored
  health to men's bodies and sanity to their minds.
  I thank you that he cared
  for all who were in pain of body and in distress of mind.
  I thank you for all doctors
    who follow in his steps;
      for all who have studied and toiled and experimented to
        find a cure for disease;
      for all who have risked their life and their health that
        others might be healed;
      for all who have skill to heal the body;
      for all who have patience to minister to minds
        which have lost their balance;
      for those whose quiet, calm strength stills men's fears,
        when they are worried and in pain.
    Give to all engaged in the work of healing
      the joy of knowing that they do the work
        of Jesus, the Good Physician.

Jesus said:
    Those who are well have no need of a physician but those who
    are sick . . . I came not to call the righteous but sinners.
                                                    Matthew 9:12, 13

    Where'er they heal the maimed and blind,
      Let love of Christ attend,
    Proclaim the Good Physician's mind,
      And prove the Saviour Friend.
    For Christ the Lord can now employ
      As agents of his will,
    Restoring health and strength and joy,
      The doctor's love and skill.

A THANKSGIVING FOR THE GOODNESS AND MERCY OF GOD, AND FOR ALL THAT LIFE HAS GIVEN AND TAUGHT

O God,
I have learned a lot
  since I came to this bed.
I have learned the uncertainty of life,
  that we cannot tell what a day will bring;
I have learned the weakness of life,
  that I am a frail creature at the best.
I have learned that I am not indispensable,
  that life gets on well enough without me,
  which is both humiliating and comforting.
I have learned a lot about you.
  I have learned to see your hand when things go badly
  just as much as when they go well;
  that the shadows are yours just as much as the sunshine.
  I have learned that
    the more I need you, the more you are there.
I know now that
  you do work all things together for good,
  and that you do love me with an everlasting love.

I too can say:
  Hitherto the Lord has helped me.

I Samuel 7:12

Every joy or trial
  Falleth from above,
Traced upon our dial
  By the Sun of Love.
We may trust him fully
  All for us to do;
They who trust him wholly
  Find him wholly true.

A THANKSGIVING FOR HOSPITALS

O God,
I thank you that there are such places as
    hospitals and infirmaries and nursing homes.
I thank you for those who have the skill
    to find out what is wrong and to put it right again.
I thank you for those
    who throughout the day and night
    attend to those in discomfort, distress and pain.
I thank you that there are places
    where the ill and the weak and the old
    are not looked on as a nuisance,
    but where they find loving care and attention.
I thank you
    not only for doctors and surgeons and nurses,
    but for all the people who do the many jobs
    which have to be done, if the work of the hospital is to go
        on –
    technicians, dispensers, dieticians,
    almoners, cleaners, ward maids,
    secretaries, typists, clerks,
    porters, ambulance drivers,
    cooks and kitchen maids.
Help me to remember
    all those who are helping you
    to make me well again,
    and to give thanks for them.

Help all those who work in hospitals to remember what Jesus
    said:
    Truly, I say to you, as you did it to one of the least of these
    my brethren, you did it to me.   *Matthew 25:40*

To comfort and to bless,
To find a balm for woe,
To tend the lone and fatherless,
    Is angels' work below.

FOR DOCTORS,
NURSES AND HOSPITAL STAFF

O God,
I ask you to bless
  all those who care for me in this hospital.
Bless the surgeons and the physicians.
I thank you
  for the knowledge and for the skill
  which you have given to them.
Bless the nurses.
I thank you
  for their cheerfulness and their patience and their watchfulness
  all through the day and night.
Bless those who cook the meals
  and who clean the wards,
  and carry out the endless administrative duties that a place like
  this needs.
Give to all who care for the sick,
  not only here but in all hospitals and infirmaries and
  nursing homes
  joy and satisfaction in their work.
And when they get tired of their work,
And a bit fed up with people like me,
  help them to remember how great a thing it is to ease the pains
  and heal the bodies of suffering men and women.
And help them never to forget
Jesus who healed all those who had need of healing.

Let me remember what the Gospel tells me about Jesus:
  That evening they brought to him many who were possessed
  with demons; and he cast out the spirits with a word, and
  healed all who were sick. This was to fulfil what was spoken
  by the prophet Isaiah: He took out infirmities and bore our
  diseases.

Matthew 8:16, 17

FOR HOSPITAL VISITORS
AND CHAPLAINS

O God,
I ask you to bless
all hospital chaplains,
and all who come to visit people
  in hospitals and in infirmaries and in nursing homes.
Give them sympathy
  so that they may really and truly enter
    into the anxieties and the fears and the pains
      of those they visit.
Give them cheerfulness,
  so that their visit
    may be like a ray of sunshine.
Give them insight
  so that they may know
    when to stay
    and when to go.
  Help them never to visit just as a duty,
  but to come because they really care
  and really want to help.
And, when they come,
  help them to bring with them,
  something of that Master and Lord
    to whom men and women and children upon earth
      came for help and healing.

May those who visit those in trouble remember the prophet's
  word:
  The Spirit of the Lord God is upon me,
  because the Lord has anointed me
  to bring good tidings to the afflicted.

Isaiah 61:1

From Thee all skill and science flow,
  All pity, care, and love,
All calm and courage, faith and hope;
  O pour them from above.

A PRAYER FOR OPERATION DAY

O God,
This is the day
   when operations are carried out.
Help those who have to go to the operating theatre today
   not to be too nervous or anxious or frightened.
Help them to trust
   in the kindness and the efficiency of the nurses,
   the wisdom of the anaesthetist,
   the skill and the knowledge of the doctors and the surgeons.
And help them to remember
   that you are just as near them in an operating theatre
      as you are in any church.
Help the rest of us who have already been through things
   to help those who have to go through them.
Help them to know that it is worth anything to be well again,
   and to remember that nothing in life or in death
      can separate them from you.
Help those at home
   not to worry too much.
We cannot help being anxious
   when our loved ones are ill.
But help us in confidence and in calmness
   to leave everything
   to the healing skill of men,
   and to your love.

Let me say what the Psalmist said:
   When I am afraid,
   I put my trust in thee.

Psalm 56:3

The Lord's my light and saving health,
   who shall make me dismay'd?
My life's strength is the Lord, of whom
   then shall I be afraid?

A PRAYER FOR A
HOSPITAL RECEIVING DAY

O God,
This is the day when the new patients
  come into this ward.
I know how they are feeling,
  uncertain, strange, apprehensive,
  nervous, worried, downright afraid.
Help me to do everything I can
  to help them.
Help me
  to try to welcome
    those who are shy;
  to try to calm
    those who are nervous;
  to try to help
    those who are afraid not to worry.
In this ward we are a lot of bits and pieces of humanity flung
  together,
  because we all happen to have something wrong with us.
While we are here
  make us one family,
  so that no one who comes in
  will be left feeling a stranger.

The Psalmist said:
  The Lord preserveth the strangers.

Psalm 146:9

In sickness, sorrow, want, or care,
Whate'er it be, 'tis ours to share;
May we where help is needed, there
  Give help as unto Thee.

A PRAYER FOR DISMISSAL DAY

O God,
This is the day
   when a lot of people in this ward
   are going to be allowed to go back home.
     And I can't help envying them.
It's not that I grudge it to them,
and it's not that I don't appreciate
   all that is done for me here,
   but home is home, and there's no place like it.
All the same, help me to be glad
   because they are glad.
There is nothing like the joy
   of meeting after separation,
and wives and husbands, parents and children,
   will be meeting again tonight.
Keep them from too much excitement,
   and from trying to do too much at first,
   and from all discouragements and setbacks.
Help me to be so good a patient,
   that I too will soon get home,
   and when the new patients come in,
help me like a veteran soldier
   to do my best to help
     those who are beginning the battle
      to be well.

Let me learn, as Paul wanted his friends to learn,
   to rejoice with those who rejoice,
   and to weep with those who weep.

Romans 12:15

   Still the weary, sick, and dying
     Need a brother's, sister's care;
   On Thy higher help relying
     May we now their burden share.

AT THE BEGINNING
OF A NEW DAY

O God,
Help me all through today.
Help me
  to be grateful for any progress
    however little.
Help me
  not to be discouraged by any setbacks,
    however disappointing.
Help me
  to be easy to help,
  so that the doctors and nurses
    may find me a good patient.
Help me
  to help others who are also going through it,
  by being cheerful and sympathetic.
Make me a good listener,
  more ready to listen to other people's troubles
  than to talk about my own.
So help me to live through today in such a way
  that at evening
  I will have nothing to regret.

Let me share the prophet's faith and gratitude:
  The steadfast love of the Lord never ceases,
    his mercies never come to an end;
  they are new every morning;
    great is thy faithfulness.   *Lamentations 3:22, 23*

We cannot tell what gladness
  May be our lot today,
What sorrow or temptation
  May meet us on our way;
But this we know most surely,
  That, through all good or ill,
God's grace can always help us
  To do His Holy will.

AT THE CLOSE OF THE DAY

O God,
Thank you
  for all that has been done for me today.
Thank you
  for the people who looked after my body,
    and my meals.
Thank you
  for the people who thought out
    the treatment that I need,
  and for the people
    who gave it to me.
Thank you for the people
whose minds took thought for me,
  and whose hands cared for me.
Forgive me, if at any time today
  I have been cross and impatient,
  unreasonable or uncooperative.
Forgive me, if I did anything
  to make the work of others harder,
  and my own recovery slower.
Thank you
  for the friendships we have made in this ward,
Specially bless and help . . . and . . . and . . .
Help me now to sleep well,
and to waken refreshed tomorrow.

Let me think of the Psalmist's faith:
  He will give his angels charge of you
  to guard you in all your ways.

Psalm 91:11

  Now God be with us, for the night is closing;
  The light and darkness are of His disposing,
  And 'neath His shadow here to rest we yield us,
    For He will shield us.